Creation

and Scientific Creativity:

A Study in the Thought of S. L. Jaki

To the memory of my father

Christopher Haffner

CREATION

AND SCIENTIFIC CREATIVITY:

A Study in the Thought of S. L. Jaki

Paul Haffner

Christendom Press

Copyright © 1991 Paul Haffner

Haffner, Paul (1954-)
    Creation and Scientific Creativity

    1. Life and thought of S. L. Jaki 2. Doctrine of creation.
        3. Science and faith.

ISBN 0-931888-41-1

Published in the United States by
Christendom Press
Christendom College
Front Royal, VA 22630

Contents

Foreword 7

Introduction 9

1. A Scholar's Portrait 13

2. The Status of Science 20

3. Pitfalls and Prospects of Science 33

4. Christ and Creation 49

5. Man's Cosmos 66

6. Jaki and his Critics 82

7. The Crucial Thrust 98

8. The Ecclesial Perspective 114

Notes 133

Publications of Stanley L. Jaki 173

Index of Names 201

Index of Subjects 204

Foreword

This work seeks to portray the contribution which Stanley L. Jaki, winner of the Templeton Prize for 1987, has made in his many publications to a deeper understanding of the relationship between Christian faith in God the Creator and modern science. The following pages owe much to many, above all to Father Jaki himself. In addition to helping me to compile a full list of his publications, he made many suggestions, concerning the development of the topic as well as details of various kinds, including the ones that relate to his Hungarian background. Since the original form of this book was a doctoral dissertation, I would like to thank Fr. Willibrord Welten, S.J., of the Pontifical Gregorian University, for his help as a moderator. I have also received valuable assistance from Fr. Gerald O'Collins, S.J., Dean of the Faculty of Theology there. Dr. Peter Hodgson of Oxford University read parts of the manuscript and made valuable comments, especially in relation to scientific questions.

Among others whose help I wish to acknowledge are Mgr. Amandio Tomas (Rector of the Pontifical Portuguese College, Rome), Mgr. Jack Kennedy (Rector of the Venerable English College, Rome), and the Franciscan Sisters of the Atonement in whose convent at Via Monte del Gallo I served as chaplain for several years. Thanks more than the written word can convey are due to my mother, Mrs. Luce Jean Haffner, and my sister, Dr. Christine Haffner. I was much helped by the fatherly good will of the late Bishop of

Portsmouth, the Right Reverend Anthony Emery, and the present Bishop, the Right Reverend Crispian Hollis. I keep a grateful memory of the generosity of the late Mr. Chauncey Stillman, President of Wethersfield Institute. May this work serve as an introduction to Father Jaki's vast researches and profound insights on the close ties between the exact sciences and the Christian theology of creation.

Rome, May 24, 1991,
Feast of Our Lady Help of Christians

Introduction

Science encourages legitimate human curiosity to know the universe and to admire and contemplate its beauty and goodness. In this way we enter into communion with God himself, who looked upon what he had created and saw that it was very good.

Pope John Paul II, "Discourse to the Pontifical Academy of Sciences," Sept. 26, 1986

For centuries the Church has proclaimed the words, "I believe in one God, the Father Almighty, the Creator of Heaven and Earth, of all things visible and invisible." If today we need to penetrate anew the profundity of this first article of the Creed, it is mainly because of the great advances made in the scientific understanding of the cosmos. Pope John Paul II had this need in mind as he urged that the mutual relations of faith and science be thoroughly reconsidered: "The issue today is no longer that of opposition between science and faith. A new period has begun: the efforts of scientists and theologians must now be directed to developing a constructive dialogue."[1]

Recent great advances in the scientific understanding of the cosmos have not resulted in a corresponding increase of reverence for God the Creator. Actually, the opposite may be the case as diagnosed by the editor of an American religious periodical: "It seems to me that the rejection of God as the Creator of the world, and therefore as the Creator of each one of us, is at the root of the rapid disintegration of of Western culture and civilization that we see all around us and that we see daily on our TV screens."[2] Perhaps this is due to a sense of power and self-sufficiency which man acquired from his greater knowledge of and control over material reality. Late-20th-century man feels tempted to look upon himself as a kind of a creator, not in the least because of irresponsible boasting of some prominent physicists that they can literally create matter, and indeed entire universes, out of nothing.

At the same time, many people are beset with fears and anxieties concerning the effects of science and technology. Man feels dehumanized by being turned more and more into a robot of his own tools. He is plagued by psychological and social problems which are often an indirect result of scientific progress. One witnesses a social disintegration on a scale never seen before. The human race, for the first time in its history, is capable of destroying itself by more than one product of its ever more penetrating study of the structure of matter, inert or living.

Faced with these contradictions, one may be tempted to take refuge in an anti-progress mentality or in a bucolic environmentalism. This would be an escape from reality as we now have it, and would undervalue the material progress which humanity has achieved though far from globally. The modern Christian should have the courage given to the Church at Pentecost to face reality as it is. Scientific development is a fact — sometimes its consequences are good, sometimes the applications are for ill. But, in order to evaluate the broader consequences of science and technology, the issue must be faced honestly. The relation of science to society is a coin necessarily with two sides, both of which must be given proper consideration. It is important to see that relation in its total cultural context, for science was born within a culture and also has given rise to a culture. An actual example of science giving birth to a culture is the way in which progress in electronics has given rise to computer graphics. As well as forming the basis of a new culture steeped in visual media and instant communication, computer graphics is most effective in facilitating further progress in science.

Can Christian faith lead us forward? Certainly, although not necessarily in every minor detail, let alone with immediate easy answers.[3] Of course, the Church has always held that there is no contradiction between faith and reason, and solemnly reaffirmed this in the latter part of the last century when science took on a new vitality.[4] Faith, in turn, has various aspects, of which the two main kinds are its attitudinal and propositional dimensions. The propositional element grounds the living act of faith in its content. The present work is concerned with the content aspect of faith for the following reasons. First, we are treating the question of how belief in God the Creator has affected culture and therefore science. While belief here too includes the sense of relational obedience, nevertheless, as being more objective, the content aspect is easier to specify even in its historical and cultural perspective. Also, it is the content aspect of Christian belief in God the Creator that can best be seen in relation to modern science taken as an objective enterprise.

As to science, it will be considered insofar as it consists of a set of propositions based on experiments, suggested by hypotheses and theories, and also in relation to the cultural context in which these propositions were interpreted. In this work, physics is taken for the prime analogue or paradigm of modern science, partly because through its mathematical mould it has achieved an exactness far superior to other branches of science.

Such is a principal reason why special attention should be given to the work of Stanley L. Jaki. One of the very few theologians who is also a physicist, Jaki is also the author, with remarkable originality, of dozens of books and scores of articles on the subject. His prominence is attested by his having been the first Catholic priest to deliver the prestigious Gifford Lectures. For his work on the relation of science and religion he received the Lecomte du Nouy Prize for 1970 and, even more importantly, the Templeton Prize for 1987. With doctorates in theology and in physics, Jaki has also extensively studied the history of science. In a sense his work is aimed at showing that the fate and fortune of creative science have always been intimately linked with the Christian doctrine of creation.

Hence the choice of the main title, *Creation and Scientific Creativity*, of this study in the thought of Stanley L. Jaki. As any title, this too implies a limitation. It allows to deal with only one, though certainly central, aspect of Jaki's thought which has other important facets. For instance, his introduction and notes to his translation into English of Lambert's *Cosmological Letters* prompted one reviewer to state that as a consequence the history of scientific cosmology during the 18th century has to be thoroughly rewritten.[5] Owing to the keen interest, during Vatican II, in ecclesiology, his doctoral dissertation,

Les tendances nouvelles de l'ecclésiologie, first published in 1956, was reissued again in 1963.

Since the present work is essentially theological, the focus will be on the theological aspects of Jaki's work on science and on its consequences for theological reflection. Those aspects and consequences are prominent in Jaki's writings. The main thrust of his work is centered on specific theses with direct relevance to the first article of the Creed. This can readily be seen from his own formulation of them: "The existence of mind as distinct from matter; the fundamental importance for scientific method of an epistemology embodied in the classical proofs of the existence of God; the limited validity or relevance of exact science or physics; the crucial importance of Christian belief in creation for the unique rise of science."[6] These four basic themes have been borne in mind in the organization of a topical and synthetic presentation of Jaki's doctrine on the relationship between faith in God the Creator and modern science.

1

A Scholar's Portrait

He brings to his work a formidable grasp of theology and science, a wide knowledge of philosophy, extensive reading of history, a mastery of half a dozen languages and awe-inspiring capacity for sustained scholarly work.

P. E. Hodgson in *Downside Review*

Stanley L. Jaki, the first Catholic priest chosen to deliver the Gifford Lectures, is one of about ten Americans to have done so, following Josiah Royce, William James, John Dewey, Reinhold Niebuhr, and Paul Tillich. Jaki gave these lectures in 1974-75 and 1975-76, at the University of Edinburgh. The invitation for the Gifford Lectures was issued to Jaki in May 1973 on the strength of his by then very impressive list of publications which earned him a world reputation as an historian and philosopher of physics.

It was as a theologian that Jaki began his work. The Benedictine Order in Hungary sent him to Rome in September 1947 to finish his theological studies, so that he might return to Pannonhalma Archabbey (which celebrates its millennium in 1996) and teach theology. He obtained his doctorate in December 1950 with a dissertation published in 1957 as *Les tendances nouvelles de l'ecclésiologie*,[1] and subsequently republished in 1963 during the Second Vatican Council. By then, Jaki had changed course somewhat by delving into his studies of the history and philosophy of science. What were the reasons for this?

13

First of all, there is a scientific strain in Jaki's family background. His mother's uncle, Gusztáv Szabó, was Rector of the József Nádor Müszaki Egyetem (Hungarian Institute of Technology) in Budapest in the 1930's. Jaki's elder brother, also a Benedictine and a graduate of the Pázmány Péter (now Eötvös Lóránt) University (Budapest), taught for decades physics and mathematics in two preparatory schools of the Benedictine Order in Hungary. He himself had outstanding teachers in mathematics and physics at the Jedlik Gymnasium, a Preparatory School run by the Benedictine Order in his native town, Györ. For three years during his student years, the Yearbook of the Gymnasium carried a book-length essay by one of the physics teachers on the life and work of Anyos Jedlik (1804-1888), a Hungarian Benedictine and the co-discoverer of the dynamo, who was also the predecessor of Lóránt Eötvös in the chair of physics at the Pázmány Péter University (Budapest).[2]

Györ — a Roman, medieval, baroque, and modern industrial town — where Jaki was born on Aug. 17, 1924, and where he grew up, instilled into him a keen appreciation for history. Upon his graduation from the Jedlik Gymnasium in June 1942, he entered the Benedictine Order and, after completing his undergraduate training in philosophy and theology, he was sent to Rome in 1947 to obtain his doctorate in systematic theology at the Pontifical Institute of Sant' Anselmo.

Following his defense of his doctoral thesis in late November 1950, he was not allowed by his Order to return to Hungary, a country subject at that time to Stalinist oppression. Nor was he allowed to remain in Europe, although he was fluent in French. He therefore accepted an invitation to Saint Vincent Archabbey (Latrobe, Pennsylvania) to teach systematic theology in its interdiocesan Major Seminary and French in its College. From the Autumn 1951 until early 1954, he taught the tracts *De Deo Uno, De Deo creante, De homine et gratia,* and *De novissimis.* As these tracts often touch on scientific questions he wished to study the latter in depth for the benefit of his students. First he delved into outstanding popularizations of science such as those written by Eddington and Jeans. He soon realized that a thorough training in physics was most desirable for the purpose. He began to attend courses at Saint Vincent College in mathematics as well as in American history and literature, to gain his bachelor of science degree in 1954. During those years he paid special attention to two famous allocutions of Pope Pius XII to the Pontifical Academy of Sciences.[3] They dealt with the proofs of God's existence in the light of modern science and had some influence on Jaki who became interested in a proof of the existence of God based on the entropy of the universe.

However, on December 9, 1953, Stanley Jaki underwent a severe tonsillectomy that deprived him for ten years of the effective use of his vocal chords. He left Saint Vincent Archabbey in July 1954, partly because he was given permission to pursue advanced studies in physics. In applying to the Graduate School of Fordham University, Jaki met its prominent physics teacher, Victor F. Hess,[4] the Nobel-laureate discoverer of cosmic rays, who himself had been afflicted with a chronic ailment of his vocal chords owing to his pioneering work in radioactivity. An affinity developed between the two also because both came from the same region of the former Austria-Hungary. Jaki obtained his master's degree in physics in July 1955 and, following his general exams a year later, he started his doctoral research in September 1956. Contrary to his wishes he could not choose for his topic a subject in theoretical thermodynamics, such as the question of entropy in the universe. He was urged to undertake, under the mentorship of Dr. Hess, an experimental work, the development of a new method for measuring the distribution of radon and thoron at the earth-air interface. After defending his thesis in June 1957, he co-published it with Dr. Hess in 1958.[5]

Meanwhile, in the late summer of 1957, along with other refugee Benedictines from Hungary, Jaki took part in establishing Woodside Priory Preparatory School in Portola Valley, California. As his impaired vocal chords prevented him from teaching, he served as bursar, with plenty of opportunity to read in the history and philosophy of science at the nearby Stanford University. Jaki wrote a dozen or so articles in those years for the *Katolikus Szemle*,[6] a Hungarian Catholic quarterly published in Rome. Those articles are an early expression of his interest in philosophical questions arising in astronomy, cosmology, fundamental particle physics, extraterrestrial life, the origin of life, and the medieval origins of science.

As the dry climate in Portola Valley caused chronic discomfort for his throat, he was allowed to return to the notoriously humid East Coast, partly because he obtained a fellowship at Princeton University (1960-1962). There he took part in various graduate seminars in the history and philosophy of science. In the Autumn of 1961, the idea of *The Relevance of Physics* came to Jaki's mind. The work, ready by the Autumn of 1964, was published by the University of Chicago Press in late 1966. Years later Jaki learned that Professor Herbert Feigl was one of the three scholars who had read the typescript for the University of Chicago Press. In his report Feigl stated that "the author displayed outstanding scholarship on every page."[7]   Professor W. Heitler (renowned for his work on quantum mechanics) recommended the work as "compulsory reading for all scientists, students, and professors."[8]

Since 1965, Stanley Jaki has been on the Faculty of Seton Hall University in South Orange, New Jersey. During the academic year 1967-68, he was associated with the Institute for Advanced Study in Princeton, New Jersey. Originally, Jaki wanted *The Relevance of Physics* to include a chapter on physics and psychology and another on physics and sociology. The material of the former chapter was included in his *Brain, Mind and Computers*, first published in 1969.[9] This work gained for Jaki the Lecomte de Nouy Prize for 1970.[10] In 1975 he was promoted to the rank of Distinguished University Professor at Seton Hall University. In 1980, he was elected Hoyt Fellow at Yale. Since 1985, Jaki has been *membre correspondant* of the Académie Nationale des Sciences, Belles Lettres et Arts of Bordeaux. International recognition for his work on science and religion came on May 12, 1987, when he received the Templeton Prize for Progress in Religion. The brochure for the presentation ceremony contains the Jury's statement: "Professor Stanley L. Jaki has offered the world in a series of highly original and learned works a reinterpretation of the history of science, which throws a flood of light on the relation of science and culture, and not least the relation of science and faith."[11]

In addition to the many works which are listed in the Bibliography, Stanley Jaki has completed many lecture tours. These have included the Olbers Lecture (Bremen, 1970), the Gifford Lectures at Edinburgh (1974-75 and 1975-76), the Fremantle Lectures at Oxford University (1977), the McDonald Lecture at the University of Sydney (1980), as well as lectures in France, Belgium, the Netherlands, Germany, Italy, Spain, Greece, Hungary, Sweden, Japan, and Australia. In the United States he served as guest lecturer in more than seventy universities and colleges. In 1983 he contributed a paper on "The Physics of Impetus and the Impetus of the Koran" to the International Conference on Science in Islamic Polity, Islamabad.[12]

In 1987 he delivered the first Wethersfield Institute Lectures, followed in 1988 and 1989 by two series of lectures at Corpus Christi College, Oxford, under the sponsorship of the Farmington Institute. In December 1988 he was invited lecturer at the Southeast-Asia Bishops' Conference on Science and Religion in Hong Kong. In 1989 he gave lectures at the Pontifical Gregorian University and the Pontificio Ateneo Romano della Santa Croce in Rome, and at the Soviet Academy of Sciences in Moscow. In the same year he received an honorary doctorate from Marquette University, one of the eight such honors that have so far been conferred on him. In May 1990 he presented an invited paper, "Ecology or Ecologism?" at the Pontifical Academy of Sciences at its Symposium, held jointly with the Swedish Academy of Sciences, on the fate of rain forests.

In September 1990 there came to him the honor in which undoubtedly he sees the main recognition of his work: his appointment by His Holiness, Pope John Paul II, as honorary member, with full rights and privileges of ordinary members, of the Pontifical Academy of Sciences. His investiture took place at the Plenary Meeting of the Academy, on October 29, 1990. It is most appropriate for this study to quote from his brief acceptance speech made on that day to the Academy:

> This great honor of becoming a member of the Pontifical Academy of Sciences comes in a context — this Plenary Session of the Academy on science and culture — which is of special satisfaction to me. As a theologian and physicist I have focused, for the past thirty years, on the history and philosophy of physics. Physics, which is the most exact form of science, becomes part of human culture not only through its discoveries — theoretical and technological — but all too often through the philosophy in terms of which it is evaluated and through the interpretation of its historical development. . . . In all that research my guiding light has been Pierre Duhem, easily the greatest among French geniuses around 1900, a genius in theoretical dynamics, in the conceptual analysis of physical theories and in discover-

ing an unsuspected phase — medieval physics — of the history of science.[13]

Clearly, Jaki makes no secret of the fact that an important influence on him has been exerted by the writings of Pierre Duhem (1861 - 1916). Jaki turned to Duhem's writings when, following his doctorate in physics in 1957, he increasingly felt that the real problems concerning the relation of science and religion belonged mostly to the history and philosophy of physics. After he had read in 1961 Duhem's biography by his daughter, Hélène,[14] he felt a "meeting of minds." In particular he was intrigued by Duhem's emphasis on the importance of the medieval period for the rise of Newtonian physics. Jaki found also most congenial Duhem's defense of Christian culture, as shown by a number of works he published on Duhem.[15] His *Uneasy Genius*, a work of about half a million words, situates much of Duhem's scientific, philosophical, and historical studies in the context of his career.[16] Most recently, Jaki published an analysis of Duhem, the scientist and Catholic, with a vast selection of texts from his writings, illustrating the coherence of those aspects in him.[17] Duhem's argument that the Greeks of old failed in science because of their belief in eternal cycles, was developed by Jaki on a vast scale in his *Science and Creation*.[18] There he accounts for the "the stillbirths of science" (a momentous phrase of Jaki's) in all major ancient cultures on the basis of the absence, in all of them, of belief in creation out of nothing and in time.

Pierre Duhem saw physics as being limited by its method to the quantitative aspects of material processes. This was the reason for Duhem's insistence on a strict distinction between physics and metaphysics. This limitation of exact science is a theme which, as will be seen in Chapter Two, Jaki explored extensively.

As regards epistemology, Jaki considers himself in the line of the methodical realism of Etienne Gilson.[19] He also follows Gilson in placing basic epistemological propositions in their historical contexts. Again, with Gilson, he stresses that the validity of commonsense truths does not derive either from scientific consensus or from commonly held opinions. Jaki also regards Chesterton[20] and Maritain[21] as important proponents, even in respect to science, of a realist account of the external world.

As to theology, Jaki was strongly influenced by the studies he made at Sant' Anselmo (1947-1950) under Dom Cipriano Vagaggini, who stressed that there is a true science not only about the general, but also about the particular, concrete, and historical. In Vagaggini's treatment, systematic theology was steeped in the history of dogma, with a proper appreciation of the historic role of Saint Thomas. Most importantly, Jaki, who went to Rome with a deep sense of loyalty for the Magisterium, refused to be swayed by incipient anti-papal currents that were carried towards the Tiber from the banks of the Rhine, the Seine, the Meuse, and the Rhone. His two books on the papacy, *And on This Rock*[22] and *The Keys of the Kingdom*,[23] are an assurance that his interpretation of science is an indirect homage to the infallible teaching authority of Peter's successors.

2

The Status of Science

Our most sublime scientific knowledge, in the final analysis, has
no other foundation than the facts admitted by common sense; if
one puts in doubt the certainties of common sense, the entire
edifice of scientific truth totters upon its foundations and tumbles
down.

Pierre Duhem, *The Evolution of Mechanics*

The phenomenology of science

The approach which Stanley Jaki takes to science has much to do
with his understanding of its phenomenology and is therefore of great
importance for having a clear idea of the light he has shed on the
relation between Christian faith in God the Creator and modern
science. He uses the word "phenomenology" for a description of the
observable phenomena of science, and not in its specialized philosophical sense.[1] For Jaki science is above all a human activity,[2] the basis
of a number of its other characteristics. He takes physics because of its
precision for the prime example of science. That he considers other
branches of science, such as biology and psychology, insofar as their
cultivators try to emulate the precision of physics, is with him a
purely methodological procedure.

In describing the phenomenology of science, Jaki focuses on
two aspects: one diachronic, the other synchronic. The first em-
braces the viable birth of science from its medieval cradle, and its
growth until the present day. The other aspect refers to science as it

stands *now*, or for the last fifty years or so. Jaki sees the development of science as a dynamic and "ongoing process"[3] and notes that "the true image of science . . . as anything genuinely human, is a mixture of achievements and failures characterized by incessant changes." In order to provide a true picture of the dynamism of science, its history must be carefully studied: "The physicist who gained from textbooks and research papers his image of physics as an intellectual pursuit in forming new ideas will be greatly amazed at the actual situation that will be unveiled to him by the history of physics." The aim of a historical portrayal of science is the "balanced presentation of the current findings and phases of science."[4]

In the diachronic appearance of science, the characteristic of *progress* is very marked. Thus Jaki notes that "the precision of exact science increased by six to ten orders of magnitude during the last hundred years." He also recalls that the distances that can now be measured are a billion times greater than a hundred years ago. This is scientific progress in its most straightforward aspect. However, science also develops in unpredictable ways, partly because its progress depends on the "sudden emergence of geniuses"[5] such as Kepler, Newton, and Einstein.

A major factor in the great recent advances of science is, as Jaki points out, the intimate relation between mathematics and physics. Yet, mathematics does not provide for physics a "logically and neatly arranged ladder for unfolding deeper and deeper layers of the physical reality." Although physics cannot therefore be an a priori process, its recent growth is exponential, owing to the effectiveness of mathematics in coping with physical problems. Partly because of this, since its "first effective or viable birth in the late Middle Ages, science has been feeding on its own findings."[6]

Another important aspect of the progress of science is that it tends toward "an ever simpler and ever more universal explanation of nature."[7] The great aim of physical science is "the overall synthesis of the scientific understanding of the universe." Part of this general aim is the seeking, within physical science, of an ever-greater precision, which "affects physics in several ways. It may establish and confirm a theory, it may pose the need of further clarification, it may reveal unforeseen cracks, and at times it may force the abandonment of a theory and impose a search for a new one."[8]

A further aspect of the diachronic phenomenon of science is that it is a purposeful activity which raises the question about its well-spring. According to Jaki an intellectual faith in the purpose and order of the universe sustains the scientist in his quest to understand the cosmos.

Considered in its synchronic phenomenology, science appears to have its own particular method which centers on the formulation of a hypothesis more encompassing than others.[9] The basis of this has much to do with the use of mathematics. Jaki bluntly states that the scientific method is "counting, measuring, and weighing," and is therefore "not about persons, personal commitments, human destiny or responsibility."[10] Nevertheless science has its own particular ethos, something which goes deeper than "usefulness or expediency." Science is a search for truth, and as such needs to be conducted in an atmosphere which is free, open, and honest.[11]   Hence science is subverted when it is made the slave of a political system, such as happened in Nazi Germany and in the Communist Soviet Union.[12]

Owing to the limitations of its method, science appears to be more streamlined than other branches of learning. Partly because of this science stretches beyond social and national boundaries. Science is not, however, a set of mutually reducible terms. It is sufficient to think of the principle of complementarity, according to which not only light but all physical entities (especially on the microscopic level) are in some circumstances best accounted for as waves, in some other circumstances as particles. Although this wave-particle duality suggests a pluralism even within the quantitative realm, it provides, so Jaki argues, no justification of a broader philosophical pluralism.[13]

Science shows an image that varies according to the viewpoint of scientists, philosophers, the media, and the general public. Jaki deplores "false images" of science[14] rooted in scientism, which is defined by him as the obstinate demand that every area of human experience and reflection be interpreted by the quantitative, experimental method of physical science. Through that demand physics becomes physicalism or the conviction that the method and concepts of physics provide the model for any science if it wants to be "exact." False images of science have a detrimental effect on other fields of human enquiry whenever the scientific method (of limited competence) is foisted on them. Scientism damages science itself: "a false adulation of physics invariably leads to its strangulation."[15]   This phenomenon can be noted both in Marxism and in Western positivism, each an example of scientism.

As Jaki points out, in Marxism (Marx and Lenin claimed to have a set of rules valid in both the natural and the social sciences), which claims to be the guardian of science and progress, scientific endeavours have to follow the "party-line" and therefore cannot remain free. For example, in the Soviet system a universe infinite in space and time must be accepted a priori, to fit in with dialectical materialism. Similarly, in Comte's positivism, which needed final scientific truths in order to usher in a final or positivist age in every facet of human life, the physics of the early 1800s was expected to remain its final form. In general, so Jaki states, "the growth of physics is necessarily stunted whenever it becomes controlled by scientism that can thrive only on a physics frozen into immobility."[16]

Jaki strongly criticizes Kuhn's basic axiom that "as in political revolutions, so in paradigm choice there is no standard higher than the assent of the relevant community." According to Jaki, science is deprived of objectivity by all those who see in it a chain of revolutions, sets of research programmes, a succession of themata, or a set of paradigms and paradigm-shifts. Jaki makes it very clear that it is helpful to study the various "images" of science only "if one faces up to the question of whether those various images are merely subjective states of the scientist's imaginative powers, or objective aspects of one and the same science."[17]

As Jaki emphasizes, a rift between man and science can arise because of images which, by falsely glorifying science, render it superhuman. In that context Jaki recalls Poincaré's denunciation of "half-science,"[18] as a construct that exclusively concentrates on the quantitative element in the fabric of human existence.

In Jaki's account the gap between man and science is further widened in the context of anti-science in its various forms. He recalls as one such example the charlatanism of E. von Däniken, who regards the Egyptian pyramids as the work of extraterrestrials. More instructive is, according to Jaki, Goethe's opposition to Newton's optics. Goethe tried to "overcome the reductionism of scientism" by offering "a reductionism in reverse in which esthetics dominated everything."[19] Naturphilosophie is still another of Jaki's examples of anti-science that invites rank subjectivism in scientific work.

Jaki further traces this split between man and science in the alienation of society from science. He deplores the fact that news-editors are often sensational in their reporting of science. This often induces the public into believing that science has arrived at "the very threshold of solving the ultimate riddle of life, of finding the ultimate constituents of matter, and of sighting the true outlines of the stellar universe."[20]

A part of the synchronic phenomenon of science is that, according to Jaki, there has developed a rift between culture and science. He defines culture as "the art of finding the true proportion in things, situations, and human affairs."[21] With considerable originality Jaki made the point that C. P. Snow, in *The Two Cultures,* did not aim to bridge the gap between scientific culture and the culture of the humanities but rather "seemed to anticipate joyfully the absorption of literary culture into the scientific." According to Jaki, every definition of culture made on the basis of scientism leads to a mechanistic approach to culture as shown by the views of C. P. Snow and T. H. Huxley. In their vision of culture there remains no logical room for "a distinction between tools and goals."[22]

To sum up, Jaki is against either worshipping or belittling science, as both attitudes disfigure man's view of science as well as of reality. The view, Jaki notes, which science has of reality is important, "for strict operationalism is just as much an extreme as mechanistic realism, and the smugness and despair they generate respectively create only an intellectual atmosphere that will widen further the gap between science and the humanities."[23] Jaki repeatedly stresses that it is a fatal mistake to see science as complete in any of the stages of its history,[24] which leads us to the next aspect of the phenomenon of science or its essential incompleteness.

The incompleteness of science

Science makes such progress that within one discipline (say, physics) different discoveries shed light on each other so as to encourage scientists to look forward to a unified theory. This convergence, Jaki warns, is not the whole story, for theory and experiments do not always point in the same direction. Sometimes "the converging lines of physics suddenly veer away from one another and new avenues open up, the direction of which no one could guess with any certainty."[25] This was the case with the advent of quantum physics, which sharply contrasted with classical physics.

Another major feature of the incompleteness of science appears through its having passed through three views of the world, namely, as an organism, a mechanism, and as a pattern of numbers. Jaki finds an essential incompleteness in each of these world views as utilized by physics.

The world, so Jaki recalls in great detail and in various contexts, was conceived as a gigantic living being in all ancient cultures, including the ancient Greeks, the Arabs and even the medievals up to a point.[26] Jaki gives a most informative and original account of Socrates' role in the development of the organismic approach in science which, incidentally, reappeared in Goethe's polemic against Newton. Socrates defended purpose with an eye on the "physics of the Ionians and of Anaxagoras, which dealt only with the succession and configuration of events."[27] By overreacting to mechanism and quantities, Socrates fomented the opposite danger, namely, "the extremist stance of seeing purpose everywhere."[28]

The organismic model offered the limited advantage of providing a unity of perspective though only by imposing a debilitating incompleteness on science. It did so by allowing only qualitative and purposive questions to be raised in scientific inquiries. The organismic view failed physics in all questions of detail and imposed a view on reality that proved itself to be unsatisfactory in the measure in which science tried to advance. In Jaki's words, man had to look deeper and "consider the beautiful display on the stage of nature a poetic disguise and look for the ultimate reality in the ugly, soulless mesh of ropes, pulleys and levers found backstage." Unfortunately, "for three centuries machines were to be idolized with as little second thought as had been the concept of organism for over two thousand years."[29]

Like its predecessor (organismic physics), mechanistic physics too became a "creed," a "state of mind"[30] and as such brought about its own demise. Incompleteness in physics was not overcome when, from the early 20th century on, physicists began to take the world as a pattern in numbers.[31] Jaki notes the extent to which pure numbers are pivotally helpful in atomic theory and the study of elementary particles. As a result, so he reports, in the late 1920's it was hoped "that theoretical physics would soon come into possession of a definitive, all-inclusive mathematical formalism." This hope was based on a type of faith in mathematical description, analogous to that which supported an organismic or mechanical world-view, even if these latter are less apt descriptions than the mathematical. Yet the all-embracing mathematical synthesis has not been found: there seem to be "mutually exclusive groups of phenomena"[32] underlying quantum mechanics and the theory of general relativity.

For Jaki, and here his originality cannot be emphasized enough, the main proof of the inherent incompleteness of the mathematical world-model derives from Gödel's theorems of incompleteness. According to them, no sufficiently broad (non-trivial) set of arithmetical propositions can have its proof of consistency within itself. From this it follows, as Jaki argued, that even in the "pure thinking of theoretical physics there is a boundary present, as in all other fields of speculations."[33] A conspicuous example of that physics is modern scientific cosmology, which cannot therefore "have its proof of consistency within itself as far as mathematics goes."[34] This means that no scientific cosmology can be true on an a priori basis.

By this Jaki does not mean that Gödel's theorems preclude the possibility of a physical theory that fits all physical phenomena. He rather means that a given cosmological theory "may be true, but never necesssarily true."[35] For Jaki the all-important implication of this is that scientific cosmology can therefore never be a threat to the fundamental contingency of the universe. Since 1966, when Jaki first set forth the cosmological significance of Gödel's theorem in *The Relevance of Physics*, there has been little response from scholars. This lack of reaction stems, according to Jaki, from the fact that "the climate of thought in our times is not at all favourable for a recognition of reason's ability to bring within sight the contingency of the universe and its *raison d'être*, its having been created by a Being truly necessary."[36]

A rejection through Gödel's theorem of an aprioristic mathematical approach to the cosmos yields a corresponding stress on the experimental nature of science. Jaki reminds us that "the mind thrives on sensory experience" and that propositions, "however abstract or mathematically esoteric, are rooted somewhere, no matter how remotely, in experience." For that reason "the replacement of theories in physics will continue as before."[37]

Jaki sees an ever receding frontier in three major areas of physical research: the realm of subatomic particles; the realm of galaxies; and quest for ever greater precision in measurements.

A century ago, atoms were considered to be the ultimate, indivisible components of matter. Then, the quality of indivisibility was attributed to electrons, protons and neutrons. Today, the physicist "prefers to compare the structure of matter to a succession of layers that, like the layers of an onion, reveal themselves only one at a time." The physicist is then faced with the question: "Will there be an end to these layers in terms of the ultimate in matter or will the process of peeling away these layers continue ad infinitum?"[38]

In answer to this question Jaki reconstructs a three-thousand-year old process of which here only its 20th-century phase can be summarized. Through J. J. Thomson's cathode ray experiments, the electron was revealed as an apparently indivisible unit. From there, it was a short step towards finding an atomic world with atoms having very small nuclei. Further complexities in the realm of atoms came into view with the discovery of neutrons in 1932. Also, following the advent of quantum mechanics, it was no longer feasible to consider atomic and subatomic particles as little billiard balls, but rather as wave-packets, which implied a wave-particle duality. Then as Dirac gave in 1929 a relativistic formulation to Schrödinger's equation, he arrived at a solution which could only be interpreted as a "positive electron," to be found experimentally in 1932. With this a new world of anti-matter opened up.

In surveying the often esoteric story of fundamental particle research of the last fifty years, Jaki registers the unfolding of very many layers of matter: "The ultimate synthesis," Jaki notes, "the rock-bottom layer of the material world, is today probably as far away as it has ever been." However he qualifies this, lest he appear to support a sort of agnostic scepticism, by adding that "the kernel of scientific truth will become better defined as time goes on."[39]

Jaki states that the "question whether physics shall ever reach the ultimate form of matter is in fact more than one question." One facet of the problem concerns how many steps would be involved in arriving at the final level of matter. The process would not go on ad infinitum, since a finite entity cannot have "an infinite number of constituents."[40] Furthermore, there is the problem that to arrive at increasingly fundamental particles, instruments of ever greater energy and therefore of greater cost are required. More importantly, he warns, the philosophical problem of the relation between mathematical constructs of the mind and reality at this level is to be faced in a way which avoids idealism.

The relentlessly ongoing penetration of ever farther reaches of the cosmos has been a process which, as Jaki argues, does not fail to convey a sense of incompleteness. Once more he proves his point by a review of history to which he contributed with important and highly original monographs.[41]

His survey of the first major phase of that story runs from the Ionians, through Ptolemy, Copernicus, and Thomas Wright to William Herschel. Although the Herschelian universe (the observable world confined to our galaxy) "displayed a uniform character not only in its structure but also in its large-scale motions and chemical composition," it fully shared in the fate of all previous world models: the "ultimate frontiers of the universe eluded man anew."[42]

A limitation of science is seen by Jaki in the lack of appropriate reaction of the scientific world to Olbers' paper of 1823 in which Olbers called attention to the paradoxical feature of the darkness of the night sky. Insufficient attention to that paradox led to the myth of one-island universe, or the idea that the observable universe is surrounded by an infinite unobservable realm of matter, a clear evidence, in Jaki's words, of an intellectual schizophrenia at work.[43]

Jaki's review of further developments aims at unfolding the failure of repeated efforts to establish the true status of the universe either in space or in time. He makes much of the failure of the steady-state theory of the universe whose proponents claimed to say the last word on the cosmos in terms of the "perfect cosmological principle," namely, that the universe must appear the same at all times and in all places.[44] Jaki is no less critical of those who see in the expansion of the universe a means of tracing it back to its very first moment. Reaching a complete view of the cosmos is possible according to him only if one ignores the incompleteness of the method of physics, or its inability to observe the nothing.[45]

Jaki takes his next major example of the incompleteness of physics from the role of exact measurements in physics. Obviously, along the three periods into which Jaki divides physics — organismic, mechanistic, and mathematical — there has been a vast increase in precision in measurements, though in a manner that cuts both ways:

it proves as well as disproves theories, in further evidence of their incompleteness. Meanwhile physicists were confronted with Heisenberg's uncertainty principle according to which magnitudes represented by conjugate variables cannot be measured simultaneously with unlimited precision. Jaki further recalls that theoretical considerations, based on the uncertainty principle, imply that there is a smallest observable time interval and a minimum of measurable extension. Such limits, he notes, should not be seen as soon to be reached.[46]

Science, as Jaki shows, is incomplete in articulating the world-view which it presupposes as well as in its theoretical and experimental progress. He further argues that science reveals its limited nature through the invariable failures whenever it is relied upon to answer questions of philosophy, ethics, and theology. Jaki categorically states that it is foolish to expect science to "solve all conceivable problems, select war strategy, predict business trends, settle the authenticity of the Pauline letters, and even compose symphonies."[47] There is no one type of knowledge which can "do full justice to the entire gamut of human experience about existence." One must not expect of science more than it is able to yield. Scientific knowledge is an integral part of human knowledge and yet it remains only a part. Like such other spheres as poetry, music, letters and politics, it can "engage only a part of man, it can satisfy only one aspect of man's ability to know."[48]

While Jaki regards science as incomplete both in its theory and practice, and in its relation to other spheres of knowledge, he avoids regarding this incompleteness as of direct theological significance. This would smack, he warns, of a naïve "God of the gaps" approach. Jaki deplores the placing of God "directly and immediately beyond the world of atoms," because any scientific step beyond the atoms would then discredit inferences to God's existence.[49] The reason for discussing the limited nature of science is rather to give a picture of its sphere of competence and its relation with other branches of human knowing, and above all to show the need for non-scientific methods in the broader quest for man's understanding of the cosmos and of himself.

The metaphysical-epistemological basis of science

Science is an intellectual activity involving man, his instruments, and the cosmos, none of which is provided by science. It is a further evidence of the incompleteness of science that its method as such cannot even assure us of the very existence of the objects it investigates. Jaki also stresses that "physics, as a way of thinking, . . . is primarily the physicists' way of thinking about their own craft."[50] He shows that physicists enhanced the incompleteness of their craft by falling prey, time and again, to extremist epistemological views. In Jaki's survey of this story, we see that no justice is done to science by two epistemologies, empiricism (also as positivism and materialism) and rationalism (also as idealism). They in turn put too much stress on matter and on mind at the expense of their rich interaction.

In Jaki's analysis of that process the starting point is Ockham's nominalism. The empiricist movement gathered further momentum through the writings on science by Francis Bacon, Thomas Hobbes, and Marin Mersenne. With Mersenne, science became less and less "a quest for understanding and a method of how to know"[51] and more and more a concern with the know-how.

A further development of empiricism came with David Hume who built his empiricism on sheer sensationism. In Jaki's graphic description, Hume took sensory impressions as so many bricks to construct a philosophical house, without resorting to some epistemological mortar other than mere habit to cement them together. For Hume there were mental states but no mind and, as a result, his method of science left no reliable means for dealing with objective reality. Positivism is seen by Jaki as an offshoot of empiricism in which facts themselves were supposed to impose the true conceptual system. While "the idealists equipped the mind with illusory wings to make it leave for ever the realm of the sensory,"[52] the positivists confined its flight within the sensory realm. The extreme case was Mach's sensationism where physics is reduced to a mere co-ordination of sensations.

The next step in Jaki's historical analysis of the epistemology of physics relates to the Verein Ernst Mach, which gave birth to the Vienna Circle. Its members shared the doctrine that reliable knowledge had to be strictly and unambiguously communicable, a quality which they granted only to quantitative or purely logical propositions. They therefore became advocates of scientism with no real reverence for science. Their chief interest related to the exploitation of science for a non-scientific purpose.[53]

As Jaki further shows, in Kuhn's historicism science is the haphazard succession of sundry paradigms which deprives science of an ontological basis, in much the same way in which logical positivists provide no ontological basis for language.[54] Jaki rejects the reduction of knowledge and language to logic on the ground that "the logician, or the philosopher who is logical by emphasis, is an advocate of solipsism."[55] Jaki rejects Wittgenstein's handling of language as one that locks the philosopher and the scientist within a self-imposed conceptual circle of logical analysis.

In the rationalist-idealist tendency, Jaki finds another extremist position which, when used in physics, imparts a debilitating incompleteness to it. He singles out Descartes, Spinoza, and Malebranche as the early representatives of this tendency. While Descartes had little use for experiments, Spinoza could not cope even with the fact that matter was a richly varied reality.[56] Malebranche essentially parted with the existence of the external world as he made it a matter of faith. His "occasionalism" left no logical room for science, which presupposes a coherently interconnected cosmos.

Jaki further illustrates the threat which rationalism poses to physics with a detailed analysis of Kant's philosophy, so often embraced by physicists who failed to note the trap it laid for them. Physics, Jaki argues, can but become devoid of meaning if Kant is right in claiming that the mind knows things by imposing its own structure on reality. After calling attention to the fact that Kant was already a-prioristic in his pre-*Critique* phase, Jaki notes that in his post-*Critique* phase, Kant held that the structure of the mind determines the structure of reality, a conclusion that undermines the need for observation and experiment: "Whatever Kant's intentions, his 'critical' work inevitably leads to the most uncritical philosophical stance: subjective idealism, if not plain solipsism,"[57] a stance impossible to reconcile with science.

Needless to say, no physicist wanted to make the method of physics utterly incompetent by endorsing the idealism of Fichte, Schelling, and Hegel. Their vagaries in matters of physical science form some of the most entertaining pages in Jaki's account of the phenomenology of physics.[58]

Jaki regards the mind as "neither an empiricist slave nor an idealist lawgiver with respect to nature, but a partner which teaches about nature by learning from it."[59] The middle ground[60] is the epistemology of classical scholastic philosophy in which the contingency of the universe means that one cannot have an a priori discourse about it, while its rationality makes it accessible to the mind but only in an a posteriori manner, that is, with empirical investigation. Jaki regards this middle road as responsible for the great scientific creativity of Newton, Planck, and Einstein. He shows nevertheless that they often held that epistemological position in an inarticulate if not unconscious manner.[61]

A firm and balanced stance in the face of these epistemological extremes is provided by a realist epistemology. As will be seen in the next chapter, the metaphysics behind that epistemology of middle ground is, according to Jaki, closely related to Christian belief in God the Creator.

3

Pitfalls and Prospects of Science

Faith in the possibility of science is *a most conscious* derivative from the tenets of medieval theology on the Maker of Heaven and Earth.

S. L. Jaki, *Science and Creation*

In Jaki's views of science as a phenomenon with built-in limitations a special place is occupied by the one which forcefully reveals the pitfalls and prospects of science. The limitation consists in the unique rise, or viable birth of science in late-medieval Europe as opposed to its repeated stillbirths in all ancient cultures. This limitation, already mentioned, will be explored in detail in this chapter because it represents the historical link to that metaphysical view of the cosmos that alone was conducive to the rise of science, after which science could feed on its own achievements. The metaphysics, anchored in belief in God the Creator, will then be examined in its relation to some propositions of modern science. To show the manner in which Jaki forges the link between Christian faith and modern science is the aim of this chapter.

The historical perspective: stillbirths and a viable birth

In his analysis of the stillbirths and the unique viable birth of science, Jaki approaches history in a way consistent with his approach to reality in general: the way of moderate realism. It corresponds to taking a middle ground between regarding history as almost every-thing (an error analogous to that of materialism) and taking history for practically nothing (an error analogous to that of idealism). He therefore rejects historicism, which is the positivist approach to history, as well as the evolutionist view of history in which the passage of time is without purpose. According to him "both metaphysics and historical reality must be taken seriously and in their entirety," and all the more so because the history of science contains a decisive truth to be uncovered: "One must show readiness to look for a lesson in all its phases, in the most developed as well in the most embryonic, and in particular to try to see whether a consistent lesson can be found in the entirety of the historical process."[1] One side of that lesson or truth is that "science came to an aborted birth in seven great cultures: Chinese, Hindu, Maya, Egyptian, Babylonian, Greek, and Arabic."[2]

Underlying all those stillbirths is, according to Jaki, an interplay of two conceptual factors that are ultimately but two sides of the same coin or currency which is not convertible into belief in a transcendental Creator who set autonomous consistent laws to the universe created by him. In terms of those two factors the universe is a huge organism about which one can only predict that it would go through endless repetitions of birth, death and rebirth. As one may expect, there is, therefore, a major difference between the approach of Jaki and that of J. Needham to the failure of the ancient Chinese in matters scientific.

The difference comes through very sharply in Jaki's evaluation of Needham who, as befits a hybrid thinker trying to be Christian (Anglican) and materialist (Marxist) at the same time, saw much good in the organismic approach which set the tone of thought, both in Confucianism and Taoism, about nature. As one may expect, Needham took lightly the endorsement by Taoists as well as Confucians of the doctrine of eternal recurrence. Jaki also exposes Needham's tactic of praising and damning in the same breath Christian belief in a truly transcendental Creator and Lawgiver, although something akin to that belief, in Needham's own admission, might have made it possible to the early Chinese to conceive the notion of genuine scientific laws.

Quite differently is the same problem handled by Jaki. He lists in detail the various organismic metaphors (mostly based on the human body) in terms of which Chinese sages tried to understand the universe. After listing the major Chinese technological feats — gunpowder, blockprinting, and magnets — he calls attention to the psychological implications of the cyclic world view and notes that "the ensuing resignation of the Chinese into practical mediocrity, though not into despair and despondency, was a matching counterpart of their moderate preoccupation with the exact period of the great cosmic cycle, the Great Year."[3] Jaki further shows that, even in modern Marxist China, the philosophical atmosphere has been hardly conducive to creative science. Despite an apparent rejection of the wisdom of ancient China, the cultural revolution of Mao Tse-tung "drew heavily on ancient Confucian and Taoist aphorisms, as if they represented the spirit of modern science."[4] Confirmation of Jaki's views can be found in the catastrophic impact of the "cultural revolution" on science in Maoist China.

Where Jaki finds a dramatic illustration of the stifling impact of belief in the Great Year on the prospect of science is ancient India, the birthplace among other things of such seminal scientific insights as the decimal notation, including the place value for zero. The Hindus of old were, however, so preoccupied with the cyclic notion of the cosmos as to assign exact figures to the length of the Great Year, dominated by the Kaliyuga or the world-age of decay. In their view "the eternal recurrence was a treadmill out of which there was no point in trying to escape."[5] Within such a view one could only weaken in one's search for truth about the physical world in the form of "theoretical generalization leading to the formulation of quantitative laws and systems of laws."[6] A similar effect is found by Jaki in the preference among Hindus of old for viewing the universe as a huge divine body.

A major proof of the anti-scientific impact of the organismic world view is found by Jaki in the Babylonian cosmogony, called Enuma Elish. The fact is particularly telling when seen against Jaki's presentation of the crudely animistic details of that cosmogony.[7] There the actual world order is so uncertain as to call for a yearly expiatory ceremony, the Akitu festival, whose participants tried to ward off cosmic disorder by immersing themselves in ritual orgy. Clearly, it is not difficult for Jaki to show that in such a milieu the practical talents of the Babylonians in collecting astronomical data, so useful later for the Greeks, and in developing practical algebra, could not have been expected to rise to a truly scientific level.

In Greece of old, science came much closer to a viable birth than it did in other ancient cultures. In astronomy and geometry the ancient Greeks went beyond the phase of description, observation and classification (this stage being exemplified by Aristotle's biology or Galen's medicine) and "moved up to the stage where the entire body of knowledge was a derivative of some fundamental postulates."[8] Jaki notes that in Greek science a very creative (yet short) period (450-350 B.C.) was followed first by a period of elaboration (350 B.C.-150 A.D.) and then by a long stagnation which came to an end around 600 A.D. Such is the story of the stillbirth of science in ancient Greece where efforts to give science a viable birth by formulating the correct laws of motion invariably failed to reach the right target.

Since the proper understanding of motion is inseparable from a correct notion of time, the clue to the stillbirth of science in ancient Greece can logically be sought by Jaki in the reflections of Greek sages on their basic framework of time-perception, the idea of the Great Year. According to Jaki, who notes that the Greek world view was "steeped in the idea of eternal cycles,"[9] the same idea posed a circular barrier to the Greek mind which failed to appreciate the linear flow of time implicit in inertial motion. Jaki further argues that infinitesimal calculus could not develop within the ancient Greek ambience, for much the same reason: For this development to take place it was necessary that time be "no longer considered as a mirror image of eternal recurrences, but rather as an uninterrupted one-dimensional flow of events."[10]

As Jaki shows through many quotations from ancient Greek philosophical writings, the cyclic notion of cosmic existence is "the very foundation of the three main cosmologies developed by the Greeks, the Aristotelian, the Stoic and the Epicurean (atomistic)."[11] In that cyclic, and markedly pantheistic cosmic view, matter and its processes were eternal. This encouraged the view of man as a mere "bubble on the inexorable sea of events whose ebb and flow followed one another with fateful regularity."[12] Despondency was one of the natural reactions to this state of affairs. The other was smugness, or the belief that one's times were corresponding to riding the crest of cultural history. The latter illusion was held by Aristotle. Some of his little remembered but revealing statements to that effect, as quoted by Jaki, counter the Marxist claim that the failure of science in ancient Greece was mainly due to socio-economic factors.

Despite the fact that by the early ninth century the Arabs had acquired all of the available Greek learning, they did not really advance it, apart from some progress made in the field of optics and geometry. They certainly fell far short of the level where science, through the formulation of the correct laws of motion, becomes a self-sustaining enterprise in coping with a physical world in which all is always in motion. The case of the Arabs, according to Jaki, is all the more noteworthy because, unlike the Greeks and other ancient cultures, they were monotheists with a firm belief in creation. Yet it is precisely some aspects of this belief of theirs that hampered them in their scientific endeavors.

One of those aspects relates, according to Jaki, to the fact that there is in the Koran "an over-emphasis on divine will in relation to divine rationality." Thus for the orthodox school of Moslem thought (the Mutakallimun, exemplified by al-Ashari and al-Ghazzali), "the notion of a consistent physical law was not acceptable because it seemed to derogate from Allah's sovereign will, which appears rather capricious in not a few pages of the Koran."[13]   The other aspect relates to the inability of many Moslem intellectuals (of the Mutazalite school) to resist the lure of Aristotelian pantheism and of its necessitarian character.

The Arabs' failure will seem all the more tantalizing if one considers that Avicenna came very close to the idea of inertial motion. If the latter's formulation fell to a Christian medieval scholar, John Buridan, it then become almost imperative to suppose that, as Jaki remarks in another context, there was in the Christian faith in creation a factor that was missing in its Moslem version. The factor was belief in the Incarnation that acted as a powerful safeguard against the lure of pantheism.[14]   According to Jaki, "the crucial insight in Buridan's discussion of impetus is a theological point which is completely alien to Avicenna's thinking."[15]

That science suffered a stillbirth even in early medieval Arab civilization and that it was a self-sustaining enterprise by the late 17th century, implies that its viable birth should be sought in a relatively brief period. The "received" view has now for three hundred years been that science arose like a phoenix during the Renaissance whose spokesmen rescued Greek science from a thousand-year long neglect. Jaki argues that this view has derived its strength "partly from the Reformers' scorn for medieval Catholicism and partly from the hostility of the leaders of the French Enlightenment to anything Christian."[16] Both groups had a vested interest in painting the Catholic Middle Ages as dark as possible. As a result neither the secularist nor the Protestant world of scholarship was ready to take notice of the monumental studies of Pierre Duhem, beginning with his two-volume *Les origines de la statique* (1905-06) and continued with the his three-volume *Etudes sur Léonard de Vinci* (1906-1913). As Jaki shows in his magisterial study on Duhem, those two works had more than amply revealed the crucial debt owed by Copernicus and Galileo (and indirectly by Newton) to some medieval scholars at the Sorbonne. Studied slighting of those works anticipated a similar attitude towards the publication, in the 1950s, of the last five volumes of Duhem's ten-volume *Le système du monde*, possibly the greatest scholarly feat by a single individual in modern times. In fact, as Jaki shows, the almost forty-year delay of the publication is a proof of that "scholarly" resistance to plain evidence.[17] Jaki's criticism does not spare, in that respect, Catholic scholarship which has still to realize the crucial importance of Duhem's heroic efforts.[18]

The key point, according to Jaki, is Buridan's anchoring his impetus theory (which implies a beginning for any particular motion) in the beginning of all motion in the first moment of creation. Buridan's creative scientific thinking owed much to his keen awareness of the solemn definition, at Lateran IV, of the age-old doctrine of creation out of nothing and in time as well as to the condemnation, on March 7, 1277, by Etienne Tempier, Bishop of Paris, of 219 "Aristotelian" propositions, some of which seemed to restrict the freedom of the Creator to create the universe except in its actual form. The decree, as Jaki interprets Duhem's admiration for that act, "expressed rather than produced that climate of thought."[19]

Within that climate of thought it was possible for Oresme, Buridan's chief disciple, to treat with impressive calm the possibility of the earth's motion. Oresme's unhesitating rejection of the Aristotelian doctrine of eternal recurrence also reflects, to quote Jaki, "the robust confidence of an overwhelmingly Christian ambience for which the once-and-for-all process of cosmic existence was almost as natural a conviction as the air one breathed."[20]

Duhem's chief interest in medieval science was that of a physicist looking for the conceptual and historical sources of the basic form, the principle of virtual velocities, of the true laws of motion. It remained for Jaki, in whom the physicist and historian of physics is coupled with the theologian, to point insistently at the theological matrix of the original formulation of the impetus theory. Jaki's theological interest also provided a much needed corrective to Duhem's one-sided esteem of Ockham, who went so far along the road suggested by the decree of Bishop Tempier as to put in jeopardy the "inherent and coherent rationality"[21] of God's creation. It was not long before Ockham upset the philosophical balance by making the nominalist distinction between "God's absolute will and ordained will."[22] It left him free to cavort in paradoxical phrases celebrating inconsistency, such as the statement that there could be starlight without stars. By overemphasizing God's absolute will, Ockham prevented the unicity of God from being accessible to the mind via reason alone. Thereafter, as Jaki notes, "the recognition of the unity of material beings, or a unitary vision of the universe, so indispensable for science, was also beyond the mind's powers."[23]

Jaki also disagrees with Duhem concerning his interpretation of Thomas Aquinas. The latter's benevolent interpretation of Aristotle did not result in a diluting, however slightly, of that all-important Christian tenet that God was able and free to create any kind of universe, or not to create at all. Duhem overlooked the utter importance of Thomas' insistence on the full rationality, that is, consistency, of creation by an infinitely rational God. It was the Thomistic balance that alone made possible the view, so important for the future of science that, to quote Jaki, "the contingency of the universe obviates an a priori discourse about it, while its rationality makes it accessible to the mind though only in an a posteriori manner."[24]

If properly heeded, that insistence, so Jaki argues, could have forestalled two mistaken developments: one was the Ockhamist, and subsequently Reformed, insistence on contingency as if it could mean that God could not set consistently valid laws to the universe. The other was the Renaissance sympathy accorded to the Greek idea of the Great Year[25] beneath which lay hidden a cosmic view riveted in the abolition of all distinct contours. The most instructive case for Jaki, in this latter respect, is the pantheistic thinking of Giordano Bruno, whose claim to "scientific expertise" is demolished by Jaki in a special monograph.[26]

Typically enough, Bruno first found an echo among the anti-scientific and crypto-pantheistic protagonists of German Natur-philosophie, a fact traced out by Jaki in careful detail.[27]   He also shows that during the Renaissance it was Nicholas of Cusa, Leonardo da Vinci, Copernicus, Tycho Brahe, Benedetti, and Kepler who represented not only the best in science but also attested "the inspiration and safeguard which faith in the Creator provided for scientific endeavour during an age that witnessed a hardly concealed desire on the part of many to bring about a 're-naissance' of classical paganism."[28]

Jaki regards Galileo as a conscious and Newton as an unconscious heir to that scientific tradition which commenced with Buridan and Oresme.[29] He also shows that   Newton's epistemology was a subconscious, or at least an inarticulate middle ground between Francis Bacon's empiricism and Descartes' rationalism.[30] For Galileo, Boyle, Newton and others "the world was rational only because the Creator was supremely rational."[31] Jaki insists that it was only in such a conceptual matrix that science could experience the kind of viable birth which is followed by sustained growth.

The next and most instructive phase which Jaki traces out in the interaction between the fortunes of science and the Christian doctrine of creation relates to the thought of Kant. Jaki unfolds in detail the little remembered fact that Kant endorsed something closely equivalent to the Great Year in his youthful, and scientifically largely worthless cosmological work.[32] He also shows the equally ignored fact that the later Kant emphatically endorsed pantheism in a context that was antiscientific to a shocking extent.[33] The manner in which all this predisposed Kant to his well-known criticism of the cosmological argument, will be discussed shortly.

After Kant, the idea of the Great Year, which had for two centuries almost disappeared from the printed page, made its return through German idealism[34] and later, and most notably, through Nietzsche's advocacy of man-centered pantheism. Once more Jaki discredits these thinkers by showing in detail the nullity of their claim that they had any competence, let alone great competence in science.[35]

Such is a brief outline of the historical landscape which Jaki presents with massive documentation as a proof on behalf of a twofold proposition. On the one hand, science suffered stillbirths in all ancient cultures, because of their being dominated by pantheism, a doctrine antithetic to the Christian doctrine of creation. On the other hand, science had a viable birth in a cultural matrix which had already been steeped for centuries in that very Christian doctrine. In other words, the philosophical consequences of this belief were able to penetrate the mentality of the scientist, so as to become almost his second nature. It now remains to examine the very metaphysics or epistemology which supports the rational recognition of creation and provides an indispensable support also to creative scientific enterprise.

The metaphysical perspective: world views and cosmology

A primary feature of all great ancient cultures was a cyclic view, epitomized in the Great Year of the cosmos, or "the notion of a world existing by itself and going through the same cycles forever in great intervals." Broad espousal of that notion has put many hindrances in the way of the scientific enterprise. A chief of those hindrances is that within the cyclic view the uniqueness of each moment is undermined. Currency may then accrue to the belief that scientific discoveries will be repeated many times as well as to the belief that events may be predicted on an a priori basis. Also, if the world is without beginning, there is, again to recall Jaki, no "encouragement to think in terms of real starting points."[36] Science could not take off as a self-sustaining enterprise without a notion of time congruent with the real world. By breaking the bondage of eternal cycles, the Christian doctrine of creation in time also provided a unidirectional view of time, most useful, as has been shown, for the prospects of the scientific enterprise.

Equally important for the fortunes of science was the discrediting, again by Christianity, of another feature of ancient great cultures, the view that the world was a large living entity. Within that animistic view every object is endowed with a mind of its own and therefore its behaviour cannot be predicted. For science to be born, Jaki warns, "nature had to be de-animized"[37] and depersonalized.[38] He also points out that in the measure in which the world is seen as the ultimate entity, man identifies "with the blind forces of nature" and finds in that identification "a relief from certain metaphysical and ethical questions."[39] Most ancient cultures were imbued with magic, in which deities are simultaneously cause and effect, which, as a chaotic situation, becomes the source of blind fear.[40]

The insistance of Christian teaching on the supreme cause restored into dignity the chain of that secondary causation which is the very object of science. The link between that secondary causation and the first cause is, however, precisely the basic assumption which constitutes the backbone of the cosmological argument, implied in Aquinas' third way. In general, as Jaki points out, all the five ways of Aquinas "embodied a stance in epistemology which, as further events were to show, contained a directive instinctively obeyed by the scientific movement." In Aquinas' proofs of the existence of God, there is a basic presupposition that man is in a "cognitive unity with nature," which is also a key tenet for creative science. The real value of Aquinas' stance was seen in clear relief after "Descartes became trapped in presumption and Hume in despair as far as knowledge was concerned." Another basic idea contained in Aquinas' proofs is the notion of the universe as "the totality of contingent but rationally coherent and ordered beings." The contingency of the universe means that there can be no a priori discourse about it. This in turn could but encourage experimental investigation of reality. Furthermore, the contingency of the universe points to the ultimate in intelligibility, which, "though outside the universe in a metaphysical sense, is within the inferential power of man's intellect."[41]

Jaki therefore roundly rejects chance as an explanation for processes in the cosmos, let alone an explanation of the cosmos itself. Making chance the ultimate explanation reduces the cosmos to less than a sheer mechanism: it empties of coherence physical processes and poses an inherent threat to the purposeful nature of science. In this connection a principal target of Jaki is the Copenhagen interpretation of quantum mechanics in general and of Heisenberg's principle of uncertainty in particular. The essence of that interpretation, Jaki insists, is not science but philosophy, indeed a philosophy of anti-ontology. Once viewed in this light, the principle of uncertainty becomes, when taken for an overthrow of causality, a cheating with real matter. For, to quote Jaki, "if the inexactitude in measurement means inexactitude in ontological causality, then in each radioactive emission a fraction of real matter, however small a fraction, becomes unaccounted for in the sense of being an uncaused entity that can come and go for no reason whatever."[42] The chance proclaimed by the Copenhagen interpretation is, according to Jaki, "a philosophical ghost residing in the shadowy realm between being and non-being."[43] Jaki makes it clear that it is a fallacy to deduce an ontological proposition from the use of a purely operational tool, a fallacy made easier by the inroads of idealism and pragmatism into scientific thinking. Jaki's sensitivity for the crucial role of ontology comes through just as well in his stricture of Darwinism whose essence is "that there are no essences except one essence which is sheer matter."[44]

The inability of physics to make exact measurements of conjugate variables on the atomic level and below was largely responsible for the fallacious inference that realism fails when it comes to the very foundations of matter. Jaki, however, insists that ultimately all scientific knowledge, including that about atomic and subatomic processes, rests on commonsense realism. Real knowledge is inseparable from knowing external reality, a consideration which, elementary as it may appear, "has been stolen from Western rationality ever since Kant made his mark."[45] Jaki is firmly in the realist tradition which he defends against prevailing idealist and operationist interpretations of science: "It is a fundamental shortcoming of science that on its exact and formal level it gives the appearance of being severed from that reality which is a vast network of events standing in a causal relation. Yet, while science may and should appear in that sense severed from reality, science becomes an illusion if that apparent severance is declared to be real."[46] Jaki makes it clear that every scientific statement is steeped in realist metaphysics, and that "the amount of metaphysics in scientific statements increases in the measure in which these statements become more inclusive."[47]

Bearing in mind that Jaki places metaphysics beyond science, but not beyond nature,[48] we now examine the chief pointers toward metaphysics which Jaki finds in modern scientific cosmology. One particular scientific finding of which Jaki makes considerable use is the 2.7°K cosmic background radiation. This furnishes a clear example of how Jaki relates science, philosophy and Christian faith in God the Creator.[49] Jaki does not make the facile interpretation of seeing the 2.7°K cosmic background radiation as an "echo from creation."[50] Rather, he sees in that radiation a proof that as far as science can look back into the past history of the universe, the latter always appears a most "specifically constructed entity."[51]

Jaki makes much of the contrast between this view of the earliest phases of the cosmos and the one made very popular by Laplace through his nebular hypothesis. The latter is saddled, according to Jaki, with an illogicality, or the claim that the actual and most specific state of the material universe can be derived from an allegedly most non-specific or nebulous erstwhile condition. Jaki also points out that such an alleged primordial homogeneity could be taken for a "natural" form of existence that needs no further explanation. Such are, according to Jaki's most original analysis of the nebular hypothesis, the reasons for its having been seized by materialists and agnostics as a foil against the cosmological argument.

Jaki therefore makes much of the fact that the various early phases of the evolution of matter show slight departures from perfect symmetry or homogeneity. He notes, with an eye on the extremely slight asymmetry in the respective amounts of matter and antimatter (one part in ten billion) that "such a minimal departure from symmetry may be more startling than a patently tilted balance."[52] This and other examples suggest that the cosmos is exceedingly specific and therefore has to be contingent on a choice among a great number of possibilities. Cosmic specificity should, according to Jaki, discourage any sober mind from "thinking that such is its only conceivable and necessary form of existence."[53] For Jaki the first main implication of the 2.7°K radiation is the striking specificity of the cosmos, which, being "peculiarly limited to a particular form, is hardly the only and necessary form of existence."[54] Therefore the universe should be regarded as contingent. Jaki's originality in developing this train of thought cannot be sufficiently emphasized.

Jaki also sees much philosophical food for thought in the fact that the specificity of the universe has put cosmic evolution on a very narrow track. Without recalling technical points discussed by Jaki in detail, it should suffice to quote his words about the impossibility for the universe to have an evolution other than it had. The universe "had a very narrow escape in order to become what it actually is." The cosmos seems indeed to have been made for man, though not in the sense in which this is taken by most proponents of the anthropic principle who seem to be caught in an idealist philosophy and are subject to Jaki's severe strictures.[55] He argues against them that the cosmos is "anthropocentric in a far deeper sense than the one which was discredited by the Copernican revolution."[56]

Furthermore (and this is the third philosophical lesson drawn by Jaki from the cosmic background radiation), that radiation, through its having discredited the steady-state theory, suggests that "physical processes, even on the all-encompassing cosmic level, represent a unidirectional once-and-for-all phenomenon."[57] Jaki, however, warns against seeing in the law of entropy a strict proof of the temporal limitedness of the universe.

The fourth philosophical point that Jaki draws from the 2.7°K radiation relates to the notion of the cosmos as a strict totality of physical things. The reason for this is the homogeneous presence of that radiation everywhere in cosmic spaces. But for Jaki the most decisive pointers in that respect come from his analysis of the theory of relativity, special and general.

While the absoluteness ascribed to the speed of light in special relativity reveals something specific valid across the whole cosmos, the latter is given a special recognition in general relativity, a point made by Jaki with striking originality. The true philosophical import of general relativity lies in its ability to give, for the first time in scientific history, a consistent or contradiction-free treatment of the totality of gravitationally interacting things.[58] Therefore, Jaki argues time and again, from the viewpoint of science the notion of the universe is a valid one, a point of utmost importance with respect to Kant's criticism of the cosmological argument.[59]

Jaki also notes that the general theory of relativity provides further data about the specificity of the cosmos. Through that theory one can obtain specific data valid for the whole cosmos, such as its curvature or space-time. This specific value determines, depending on whether it is a small positive or a small negative quantity, the net of permissible paths of motion. In the former case, the universe is spherical; in the latter case its total matter is distributed in a hyperbolic space-time, analogous to a saddle with no edges but with well-determined slopes. Jaki, who wrote extensively on the paradoxes of an infinite homogeneous universe,[60] can therefore authoritatively note that "the only possibility which is excluded is Euclidean infinity whose curvature is 0, an age-old symbol of non-existence."[61]

According to Jaki, the universe looks "no less specific than a garment on the clothier's rack, carrying a tag on which one could read if not its price at least its main measurements."[62] Such a tag, in Jaki's words, "cannot help evoke the existence of a dressmaker,"[63] because there is no need for the garment to be of a particular size. Analogously, there is no scientific reason why the universe has to have the overall specifities established about it by modern scientific cosmology. Consequently, those specifities can be taken for so many pointers of cosmic contingency which in turn can legitimately be used as a ground for invoking the existence of a Creator.[64]

For Jaki, all science is cosmology in that each basic scientific law "reveals something all-encompassing about the universe."[65] Hence important metaphysical consequences are implied in choices of a physical view of the origin of the world. In the steady-state theory, the spontaneous appearance of hydrogen atoms was proposed as an emergence out of nothing, but without a creator. The theory was formulated to "secure for the universe that infinity along the parameter of time which it had already lost along the parameter of mass and space."[66] Jaki notes that several champions of the theory openly professed that very atheism[67] for which the eternity of the universe is a basic dogma.

The oscillating model of the universe has also been used by those who ascribe eternity to the universe by claiming that its present expansion is but a part of an expansion-contraction cycle that would repeat itself an infinite number of times. They usually overlook the fact that, owing to the law of entropy, each subsequent cycle has to diminish in intensity. Consequently, unless one arbitrarily postulates an infinite energy reservoir for the universe, the oscillating universe turns out to be a variation on the single expansion model with its plethora of specifics.[68]

For Jaki, the scientific cosmological model most obviously pointing to the reality of creation is single-expansion, which is also the scientifically most reliable.[69] Jaki does not, however, recommend a peremptory choice between the finite oscillating model and the single-expansion model. Instead he calls attention to deeper indications which arise in either of them about the specificity and contingency of the universe. Such indications constitute what may be called the metaphysics implicit in modern scientific cosmology.

Jaki notes four essential properties of the universe which make scientific endeavour possible. First, the cosmos has an objective existence and reality independent of the observer. This is supported by the fact that, to quote Jaki, "man through his consciousness is always in touch with a reality existing independently of him."[70] If this were not the case, man would not be seeing the world "but only his own footprints."[71]

Second, the material entities in the universe must have a coherent rationality, the basic condition of their investigability. All those entities must therefore be subject to laws which can be expressed in a quantitative framework and "must have a validity which transcends the limits of any time and location."[72]

Third, for science the universe has to be one, a true cosmos. Only then can the consistent interaction of things, which is the very basis of physical laws, be maintained. Therefore no credence is to be given to the multi-world theory according to which there are as many universes as there are observers. For, as Jaki asks, how then can one observer get out of his own world to communicate with another observer?[73]

Fourth, the very specific form in which the coherent whole exists cannot be considered as a necessary form of existence. As was shown earlier, Jaki proves this through his cosmological extension of Gödel's theorems. Thus Jaki states that "whereas General Relativity forces us to admit the realistic character of the notion of consistently interacting things, as a valid object of scientific cosmology, the application of Gödel's theorem to cosmology shows that a disproof of the contingency of the universe is impossible. The mental road to the extracosmic Absolute remains therefore fully open."[74]

The contingency of the universe is crucial in Jaki's thought, and he defines the meaning of the word "contingent" as follows: "Contingent, that is, dependent on a factor outside the set of parameters that determine the scientific handling of the problem or configuration. In case of a configuration which is equivalent to the total interacting mass, or the universe, the factor in question can only be a metaphysical factor." Such a meaning of "contingent" is essentially different from its being taken equivalent to random, haphazerd, or accidental.[75] For Jaki, "contingency" means strict dependence on an another factor, be it a conscious choice, an idea very different from chance. He is not one of those theologians who use the word contingent as an evasion of causality in order to find loopholes for God's miracles.[76] According to him "contingent universe and a created universe are two sides of the same philosophical coin."[77]

The characteristic of contingency is implied, according to Jaki, in the overall boundary conditions which make that coherent whole which is the universe. Just as boundary conditions are the mark of any existent, so is the universe marked by such conditions. While science may reduce the actually known cosmic boundary conditions to some others, not yet known, regress to infinity is hardly a logical road even for science and certanly not for philosophy. Those boundary conditions are the signs of the limited perfection of the universe and the very pointers towards its createdness. This means, for Jaki, that Aquinas' five ways are essentially one way, "the way from contingency."[78]

This discussion had for its aim a reconstruction of Jaki's portrayal of the cosmos, with an eye on science, as the totality of consistently and most specifically interacting entities, a totality of contingent but rationally coherent and ordered beings. Included in that aim is a reconstruction of Jaki's portrayal, again with an eye on science, of the connection between science and realist epistemology. Jaki's understanding of the cosmos provides one half of his construction of the arch that connects science and religion. The other half is provided by his reflections on the dogma of creation, the topic of the next chapter.

4

Christ and Creation

> The doctrine of Incarnation throws into powerful relief not only
> the dogma of creation, but also the dogma of a special course of
> Providence across history.
>
> S. L. Jaki, *Cosmos and Creator*

It was shown in the previous chapter how science arose within
a specific historical and philosophical framework and bears witness to
it. Here we consider those particular elements of the Christian
doctrine of Creation which, in Jaki's view, gave rise to an epistemology necessary for the unique viable birth of science. The Christian
view of Creation derives from a Revelation committed to a divinely-
authorized Magisterium as a guarantee of the authentic interpretation
of Scripture and Tradition. After discussing the scriptural data
emphasized by Jaki, we examine the development of the Christian
doctrine of creation in terms of his emphasis on the Redemptive
Incarnation as the source of the unique vitality of that doctrine.

The scriptural vision of creation

Jaki traces some main lines in which the Old and New Testament
picture of God the Creator is established. As a result he places all
religions in two categories: "In one there is the Judeo-Christian
religion with its belief in a linear cosmic story running from 'In the
beginning' to a 'new heaven and earth'." In the other are "all the

49

pagan religions, primitive and sophisticated, old and modern, which invariably posit the cyclic and eternal recurrence of all, or rather the confining of all into an eternal treadmill, the most effective generator of the feeling of unhappiness and haplessness."[1]

Jaki makes it very clear that there is a world of difference between creation as portrayed in Genesis and in Babylonian lore. The difference is all the more remarkable because the Israelites had the same view as their neighbours of "a flat earth floating on water" and of "a firmament resting on columns located at the extremities of dry land." Also, the Hebrew way of thinking was moulded, "as was the case with their great and small neighbours, by the same huge geographic unit stretching from the Euphrates to the Nile valley."[2] The similarity ends there. There is, Jaki insists, a marked contrast between the first chapter of Genesis (composed in post-exilic times) and Enumah Elish, the Babylonian creation story. In the first chapter of Genesis, "there are no infighting gods, no gory dismemberment of a divine mother, no threat of collapse."[3] A "nondescript chaotic material (*tohu vabohu*)"[4] is used by the Creator in Genesis 1, but it is not symbolic of either a divine principle or of an evil force on the same level as God. In Genesis 1, the chaos is wholly subject to God, as are "all general and particular features of the world which are called out of the chaos by his sovereign command."[5] However, the notion of a creation out of nothing came later when Hebrew culture had to interact with a Hellenism for which the world was divine and eternal.

The action of God in creating is conveyed by the Hebrew word *bārā*. This word, which literally means to carve (split or separate), is used throughout the Old Testament to denote an action which is proper to God as his supreme privilege.[6] This word took on such a particular colour because man realized that God's action needed to be described in a special way. The word *bārā* forms, therefore, an incisive part "of that uphill trend in conceptualization toward ever more refined and categorical statements about God, the Maker of heaven and earth."[7]

Jaki finds a sharp contrast between Genesis 1 and Enumah Elish also in that the former makes it clear that God's creation is unreservedly good. Moreover, "Genesis 1 reveals a plainly objectivist thrust by the fact that it is not God's action as such which is declared to be good but the product of his actions."[8] In Genesis 1 God is responsible for each and every part of the universe, for "heaven and earth."

In Enumah Elish, creation is the result of a life-and-death struggle within the family of gods. There the savage dismemberment of Tiamat's body "provides the material for the various parts of the actual world"[9] which is then shaped by Marduk, the strongest of many gods and goddesses. A further overall difference, according to Jaki, between Genesis 1 and Enumah Elish is that the main message of Genesis 1 is "not so much about the world as about God and man,"[10] while that of Enumah Elish lies more in details about uncoordinated cosmic forces personified in mythologies about the genesis of gods.

Genesis 2, which contains the second account of creation (and was written much earlier than Genesis 1), is, in Jaki's view, "hardly a cosmogony in the usual sense of the word." Its author moves quickly over nature to the making of man by God. Though the account is primitive, it does not make God a part of creation. The complete conceptual distinction between God and creation appears, through the use of the term "creation out of nothing," at a much later stage of development. However, already in Genesis 2 there is only one ultimate source of power, one effective cause. There is not even an indirect hint there about an infighting between gods or about a clash between equal and opposite forces of spirit and matter, good and evil, that characterize all Near-Eastern stories of creation contemporary with Genesis 2.

Jaki notes that the scriptural world-view of Genesis 2 served as a unique inspiration for such later work as some of the earliest psalms, which are a "poetical counterpart" of Genesis 2. Psalm 8 stresses God's power over everything: "How great is your name, O Lord our God, through all the earth! Your majesty is praised above the heavens." Man shares in this power of God: "Yet you have made him little less than a god; with glory and honour you crowned him, gave him power over the works of your hand, put all things under his feet." In Psalm 19, creation manifests the power and glory of God who made it: "The heavens proclaim the glory of God and the firmament shows forth the work of his hands." There is a "fusion of Cosmos and Covenant" almost in that same logical order in which the former precedes the latter, so that He who is Lord of nature is also Lord of the people He has chosen. This order is a backbone of the spirituality of the Old Testament as shown, for example, in Psalms 23 and 24. Psalm 24 begins with a statement about the sovereignty of

God over all creation: "The Lord's is the earth and its fulness, the world and all its peoples." Then it proceeds to the demands made on those who are bound in solemn covenant with God. The "worthless things" of Psalm 24 are the pagan idols of surrounding nations. Idolatry was the worst crime in the Old Testament, for the absoluteness of Yahweh's rule could not coexist with "any pantheon of gods" which, however, posed an ever-present temptation to the Hebrews. Isaiah feels the need to condemn Jewish idolatry in proof of the fact that there were times when idol-worship seemed to gain the upper hand in Israel. Yet, after the exile in Babylon, despite the exposure to paganism, "Jewish monotheism emerged from the cauldron of captivity in a far more robust and in a far more incisive form."[11]

The Old Testament contains a vision in the transcendence of God which fosters a confident outlook on the world and on nature. This confidence reveals itself most persuasively in the conflict between Jewish faith and Hellenistic ideology by leading to a clear enunciation of belief in creation out of nothing. This belief is graphically expressed in the story reported in the Second Book of Maccabees where the mother of seven sons enjoins martyrdom on her seventh son with the words: "I implore you, my child, observe heaven and earth, consider all that is in them, and acknowledge that God made them out of what did not exist" (2 Mac 7:28).

The Wisdom literature proposes the Hebrew view of Creator and creation by taking into account some Hellenistic trends. The orderliness and rationality of the universe is depicted with a reliance upon Greek philosophical and scientific concepts: "You ordered all things by measure, number, weight" (Wis 11:20). The Book of Wisdom also contains a very clear statement concerning the possibility of arriving at knowledge of the existence of God from a contemplation of what he has created. The passage to which Jaki attributes much importance is Wisdom 13:1-5, where the basic principle is that "through the grandeur and beauty of the creatures we may by analogy contemplate their Author." Thus idolatry is inexcusable, for "if they are capable of acquiring enough knowledge to be able to investigate the world, how have they been so slow to find their Master?" (Wis 13:5). As Jaki shows, Hebrew faith in God, the Maker of heaven and earth, emerged in a stronger form through its rejection of Babylonian mythology and through its repudiation of Greek pantheism. As that faith grew in its directness, it also exuded more and more confidence, a feature that was to be greatly reinforced in New Testament times.

In Jaki's historical method, the teaching of the New Testament is divided into two phases: one is centred on the teaching of Christ, the other on the Apostles' reflection on that teaching. In Christ's teaching, which fully endorses Old Testament monotheism (Mk 12:29-30), the doctrine of creation appears briefly but emphatically within a soteriological context: "I bless you, Father, Lord of heaven and of earth, for hiding these things from the learned and the clever and revealing them to mere children" (Mt 11:25). While in the same context the doctrine of Trinity is foreshadowed with a reference to the perfect unity between Christ and the Father, Christ fully approves the classic statement of Old Testament monotheism: "Listen, Israel, the Lord our God is the one Lord, and you must love the Lord your God with all your heart, with all your soul, with all your mind and with all your strength" (Mk 12:29-30).

The clash between Christianity and the Graeco-Roman world was about monotheism, which was also a question about creation. Saint Paul stresses to the Christians of Corinth in connection with left-over sacrificial food that "for us there is one God, the Father, from whom we exist" (1 Cor 8:6). Saint Paul had insisted that there "is no god but the One" (1 Cor 8:4). Paul's message in the speech on the Areopagus was firmly rooted in faith in God the Creator "who made the world and everything in it" and is "himself Lord of heaven and earth" (Acts 17:24). Paul then moves on to condemn idolatry. He echoes the vision of the wisdom literature of the Old Testament when, to show that it is inexcusable to worship idols, he states that man can come to an appreciation of the existence of God the Creator through his creation: "Ever since God created the world his everlasting power and deity — however invisible — have been there for the mind to see in the things he has made" (Rom 1:20). Now in order for there to be a possibility of arriving, through a reflection upon creation, at the existence of God, this creation must be a rational and coherent whole, or a universe. To recall Jaki's statement, "our faith can hardly become that *logikē latreia* which Paul (Rom 12:1) wanted it to be . . . if the notion of the universe is an essentially false notion."[12]

At the heart of the Christian message stands the person of Christ, who is "the image of the unseen God" (Col 1:15), and he "has become our wisdom, and our virtue, and our holiness, and our freedom" (1 Cor 1:31). Jaki makes it clear that "the Christian certitude about the rationality of nature, about man's ability to investigate its laws, owes its vigour to the concreteness by which Christ radiated the features of God creating through that fulness of rationality which is love."[13] Christian rationality was something very different from the Greek variety, for the Greeks tended either to extreme mechanism or to pan-teleologism (the stance which saw purpose everywhere). From Socrates onwards, it was the problem of pan-teleologism which prevailed, bringing with it a cosmology which was "a mixture of rank subjectivism and inescapable determinism." Lacking in the Greek conception of the rationality of the cosmos was an understanding of the freedom of man and the contingency of things. "Conviction on both points was secured only by Christianity for which the freedom of man is an indispensable tenet," as is also "the contingency of a world which is created."[14]

According to Jaki, the crucial contribution of the New Testament to the doctrine of creation is pivoted in the efforts of John and Paul to safeguard monotheism by attributing to Christ the work of creation, a work most specifically tied to the Father in the Old Testament. Such is the gist of his quoting Saint John's portrayal of Christ in whom "all beings came to be; not one being had its being but through him" (Jn 1:3). The same is true of his quoting Paul: "For in him were created all things in heaven and on earth: everything visible and everything invisible; . . . all things were created through him and for him" (Col 1:16). This notion of creation through Christ eliminated the specter of a duality between the Father and the Son while the portrayal, specific to John, of Christ as the "only-begotten Son," posed a powerful barrier within Christianity to those inroads which pantheism made within other forms of monotheism. To this latter point which is emphasized on more than one occasion in Jaki's writings, we shall return shortly.

Creation in Christ supports the idea of new creation in the New Testament where Christ is the principle through whom all things are re-made, for "all beings have a higher destiny which is expressed by their trend toward him."[15] With an eye on two passages in the Apocalypse, Jaki shows the unity of "the very first words of God" creating heaven and earth with "the last words of God"[16] that relate to the creation of a new heaven and a new earth (Rev 21:1 and 5-6).

The covenant which began in the creation of the world is therefore completed in the new Jerusalem. Jaki thus links the ways in which God acts in creation and in history: "The uniqueness of salvation history became the shield protecting the uniqueness of the history of the cosmos and ultimately the doctrine of its creation out of nothing."[17]

That uniqueness was clearly incompatible with a system of "endless cycles and blind repetitions." Belief in the God of the creation and the covenant was to foster the opposite, namely, a linear view of the history of the cosmos, which in turn became the leaven for the birth of modern science. In what follows we shall see how Jaki illustrates the fermentation of that leaven in the early centuries of the Church's history and how the dogma of creation out of nothing was formulated, with all its consequences for metaphysics, culture, and science.

The vision of creation in Christian tradition

The belief of the early Church in God the Creator was deepened in the course of the centuries and more precisely formulated, often as as a reply to challenges to it. Jaki's chief interest in that development relates to the appearance of cyclic pantheistic world-views in heterodox teachings and to the Church's resolute opposition to these world-views, an opposition pivoted in strict adherence to the dogma of the Incarnation.

Jaki's first major illustration of that resistance relates to Saint Irenaeus, who stressed creation out of nothing and denounced the idea of eternal recurrences as embodied in gnostic teachings about reincarnation. Eternal recurrences were rejected by Saint Hippolytus, a disciple of Irenaeus, as he opposed many bizarre cosmogonies. The same recurrences were, as Jaki shows, the background-target as Clement of Alexandria rejected idolatry, which for Clement was a "mental enslavement to the blind forces of nature." It is not surprising that Clement regarded the universe as a harmonious unity and held faith, as supported by natural reasoning about that universe, to be of special value.

Cosmology sets the framework of Jaki's reflections on Origen's work. He shows Origen to be under oriental influences in proposing the doctrine of successive worlds, as a means of ultimate purification even for the most wicked. A further example of oriental flavour is present in Origen's idea of the *katabolē* "or the explanation of actual material existence as a result of gradual deterioration from higher levels of being." Through such details, which have not failed to cast suspicion on Origen's orthodoxy, he tried to "assimilate into a Christian synthesis everything that appeared to him grandiose in cosmological speculations."

Still, as Jaki notes, Origen's *katabolē* is not an "inexorable treadmill." There is a goal in view within Origen's vision, namely, the restoration of all in Christ. This redemption in Christ as a unique event puts a stop to "any possible flirtation with the idea of eternal and purposeless cosmic cycles."[18] Origen made it clear that if there were an endless repetition, "then it will happen that Adam and Eve will again do what they did before, there will be another flood, the same Moses will once more lead a people numbering six hundred thousand out of Egypt, Judas also will twice betray his Lord, Saul will a second time keep the clothes of those who are stoning Stephen, and we shall say that every deed which has been done in this life must be done again."[19]

Jaki shows that the same linearity is very pronounced in Origen's dispute with Celsus. In opposing Celsus, Origen stressed that matter was good, not evil, and that there would be a repetition of all of Greek history if there were eternal returns. Origen made it clear that the history of salvation was a once-and-for-all affair; otherwise the focus of all history, the Christ-event, would be endlessly repeated. Also, if history consisted of eternal returns, it would be impossible to influence history: "The same people will be Christians in the determined cycles, and again Celsus will write his book, though he has written it before an infinite number of times."[20] Moreover, Origen showed the opposition between the Christian doctrine of the resurrection and a world-view involving eternal returns, for resurrection is such as to transform the individual while maintaining a continuity with respect to his identity.

For Jaki the most important patristic figure as regards the contrast between the Christian doctrine of creation and pagan cosmogonies is Saint Augustine, who made the greatest impact on medieval thought. The chief source of Augustine's doctrine on creation is his *De civitate Dei*, especially its books XI and XII. Mankind and the cosmos are on a meaningful course towards fulfilment in Augustine's vision, and all creatures are dependent on God the Creator's redemptive act. Augustine rejects the eternity of the world, as this notion is linked with an eternal principle of evil in the Manichaean vision with which he was well acquainted. Rather, the universe is good and history is non-cyclic; otherwise the Christ-event would be repeated and would lose thereby its exclusive value of uniqueness. He also showed how an eternal cyclic view would paralyze Christian piety in this life and undermine belief in an eternal life to come: "If they maintain that no one can attain to the blessedness of the world to come, unless in this life he had been indoctrinated in those cycles in which bliss and mystery relieve one another, how do they avow that the more a man loves God, the more readily he attains to blessedness, — they who teach what paralyzes love itself?"[21]

Augustine held high the view of the cosmos in which order and measure prevailed, and was not shy to give reason its due in the task of interpreting the scriptures. Jaki notes that Galileo, in his "Letter to the Grand Duchess Christina," used texts from Augustine and other Fathers "to vindicate the simultaneous pursuit of knowledge and of an eternal happiness."[22] In Jaki's view, the main considerations stressed by Augustine concerning creation greatly strengthened the impact of the Christian gospel on culture in terms of a special vision of man's capabilities: "A man with a restored sense of purpose, a man with an ability to discern intelligible patterns in the universe, a man aware of the vital difference between knowledge and happiness, a man confronting an external world not as an a priori product of his mind but accessible to the light of reason which itself was a participation in God's mind."[23]

Another Father whose views Jaki recalls in detail is Boethius, as one second only to Augustine in his impact on the medievals. However, Jaki focuses more attention on one of Boethius' contemporaries, John Philoponus, the author of most intriguing reflections on the cosmos. Philoponus' *De opificio mundi*, written after his conversion to Christianity, deals in an elaborate manner with the biblical account of creation. There he countered Theodore of Mopsuestia's view that the heavenly bodies were moved by angels, implying instead that they were given a certain kinetic force by God in the beginning. This is Jaki's introduction to his remark that while Philoponus agreed with much of Aristotle's views about the physical world, "wherever Aristotelian physics and cosmology seemed to encroach on the

Creator's prerogatives or on man's proper relation to his Creator, Philoponus instinctively parted ways with Aristotle." Hence Philoponus rejected the divinity of celestial matter and eternal motion as parts of a pantheistic world-picture. Jaki regards Philoponus as a forerunner of Buridan and Oresme (and thence of Galileo and Newton) in their view of inertial motion. Jaki recalls Philoponus's statement from his commentary on Aristotle's physics, that projectiles move through the air "not because the air keeps closing in behind them, but because they were imparted a certain [quantity of] motion."[24]

For Jaki, Philoponus is a clear example, during the Patristic period, of one in whom Christian belief in God the Creator beneficially influenced views about the scientific interpretation of the created world. Jaki finds the patristic period as fairly balanced in its understanding of the scriptural idea of creation. He finds a considerable contrast with later ages which "under the impact of the Reformation came heavily under the sway of biblical fundamentalism, a far cry from the way in which Augustine of Hippo, Gregory of Nyssa, Basil the Great, to mention only a few, interpreted the biblical notion of creation."[25]

In their opposition to heresy (especially Gnosticism) on the one hand and to paganism on the other, the Church Fathers gradually clarified the basic terminology in which the doctrine of creation was conveyed. In Jaki's portrayal of this development, the first step relates to the Greek and Latin versions of the verb "to create." In Christian times, both versions underwent a development somewhat analogous to that of the word *bārā* in the Old Testament. It was necessary to attach to the word "create" a specific meaning with which it was not initially endowed, in order to convey the special nature of God's action in creation. The original meaning of *creare* was nothing more than "to do, to produce, to fashion (coming from the Latin *facere*), to make." The word *creare* "had, as a derivative of *crescere*, only the meaning of making something to grow." The word *genesis* also had a great fluidity of meaning.[26] The Latin expressions *creare* and *facere* and the Greek *poiein*, heavily used by the Church Fathers, did not exclude the sense of creation taught by the Christian gospel. Yet the original meaning of the word *creare* (and of its ancient Greek and Latin synonyms) had to be clearly qualified in order to teach "concisely the difference between non-being and being."[27]

The second step emphasized by Jaki relates to the beginning of the cosmos as part of Christian tradition, incompatible with Plato's concept of an eternal universe. Nor could Christianity follow Plato and attach the word "begotten" to the universe, since this word had already been used to express the relation of God the Son to God the Father. As Jaki notes, "it was impossible to load the same word with two meanings so different as coming into being out of nothing (the origin of the world) and the eternal birth of a Son consubstantial with the Father." Thus the Christian idea of creation could not be attached to the words "to generate" and "to beget" which was all the more fortunate as the Gnostics regarded the world as an emanation from God and were fond of the expression "to beget the world." Tellingly, the Arians, sympathetic to neo-Platonist emanationism, also preferred to rely on such expressions as "to generate" and "to beget" whenever they they confronted the problem of Christ's role in the creation of all by the Father.

A similar semantic enrichment was in store for the word "to make" as in itself it would not make it clear that the undifferentiated material (chaos, *tohu vabohu*) was also created from nothing. "The thread which helped Christian orthodoxy out of the etymological labyrinth was provided by the now all too well-known expression *ex nihilo* (out of nothing) which was attached to the words *facere* (to make), *condere* (to establish), and *creare* (to make grow)." Inspired by the expression "God made them [i.e., heaven and earth] out of what did not exist" from the Second Book of Maccabees (7:28), the author of the Shepherd of Hermas stated of God the Creator that "he made everything from what was not existing to exist."

Together with that author, Aristides and Saint Theophilos of Antioch, began to use the Greek expressions *ek tou mē ontos* ("from the non-existing") and *ek ouk ontōn* ("from those not being"). Tertullian in turn introduced the concise Latin forms *ex nihilo* and *de nihilo*. The Christian notion of creation out of nothing contrasted sharply with the pagan Greek scorn for that expression which, as Jaki recalls, "occurs only half a dozen times in the vast corpus of classical Greek literature."[28]

The definition, at Lateran IV in 1215, of the dogma that the world was created out of nothing and with time[29] merely confirmed, so Jaki insists, the long-standing climate of thought described above. Related to the *ex nihilo* element in the dogma of creation is the

Council's assertion that the universe was created *cum tempore*. In reaction to the pagan views of the eternity of the world, Christian thinkers of the early centuries produced "a great variety of philosophical proofs of its temporal character."[30] According to Jaki, the doctrine of creation in time is the pivot upon which hang all the other articles of the Christian creed: "Whenever the meaning of creation in time is weakened, let alone eliminated, the meaning of all other tenets of the Christian creed become weakened or eliminated. Those tenets — Fall, Incarnation, redemption, the growth of the Kingdom of God, eschatology, final judgment — presuppose not only creation out of nothing but also a creation in time because all those tenets refer to events in time which alone can constitute a sequence which is salvation history."[31]

However, as has been seen, Jaki does not regard the 2.7°K cosmic radiation as a pointer to the moment of creation, for "no law of physics can ever be construed so as to have for its reference point that very nothing which is implied in that only true creation which is creation out of nothing."[32] Jaki holds that the notion of creation in time is also outside the reach of philosophy. He thus endorses the view of Aquinas that "neither the eternity, nor the temporality of the universe can be demonstrated on the basis of reason alone." Saint Thomas' view (that creation in time is solely a truth of revelation) diverged from that of the entire tradition from Saint Augustine to Saint Bonaventure, which held that the temporality of the universe could be demonstrated by reason.[33]

Bishop Tempier's decree of March 7, 1277, discussed in Chapter Three, is a further example, for Jaki, of medieval insights about the Christian dogma of Creation. The bishop wished to stress the difference between the Aristotelian prime mover which is neither free nor a creator and "the Christian God, or the Jewish God, or the Muslim God, who creates but is not forced to create."[34] The Christian doctrine of God the Creator implies a cosmos which is not necessary, for not only was God free not to create it, but he could have created it otherwise. The cosmos is thus contingent and cannot be fathomed by a priori reasoning; rather, it must be approached by a posteriori experimentation. This, as has been seen, is a notion of crucial importance for scientific stimulus.

The *ex nihilo* and *ab initio* nature of God's creative action was to be reiterated at the First Vatican Council against the errors of materialism and pantheism which enjoyed a new vogue at that time. In addition, Vatican I stated the absolute freedom of God to create, and made clear, against fideism, the possibility of arriving at God's existence through a rational reflection upon creation. As Jaki states: "The council, in line with a tradition almost two millennia old, could but insist on the very foundation of that relation which is man's ability to see the reasonability of revelation, which in turn is inconceivable if man is not able to infer from the world surrounding him the existence of its Creator."[35]

Jaki also makes much of the fact that the cosmos will have an end as well as a beginning. He points out that, in the Apostle's Creed, which fused biblical doctrine and the main preoccupations of the early Fathers (namely, belief in a personal Creator of all, a creation out of nothing, the strict immateriality of the soul, and the resurrection of the body), the Creator is "the source of an absolute beginning and of an absolute consummation for man and cosmos alike."[36] Furthermore, Jaki stresses that creation is good, refuting any kind of dualism which would set good and evil on the same footing; often this tendency would regard matter as evil and on the same footing as God, the principle of good. The Christian teaching on creation out of nothing and with time safeguards the complete omnipotence of God. This in turn implies that the presence of evil in the world is not an equal and opposite force to the power of God.

Jaki emphasizes time and again that the dogma of creation bears on all other dogmas and themes; it is the logical and ontological basis for the entire Christian Creed. As Jaki states: "Without Creation, and a Creation by God who is Father, there is no possibility of a discourse about Incarnation, Redemption, and final Consummation in a New Heaven and Earth, the great prophecy of the Creed." The space and time which came into being at creation constitute the means through which God acts in history and in which man responds to God's action. It is unfortunate therefore that the theology of creation has been neglected: "The theology of creation has been for many decades a stepchild in comparison with a large number of theological topics centering mostly on the notion of the Church."[37]

Creation and other dogmas

For Jaki, "original sin as a perspective of origin is inseparable from the perspective of the absolute origin of all in the beginning."[38] He notes that both creation and original sin are vindicated by science today and also recalls Chesterton's remark that, of all Christian dogmas, original sin is the most empirical. Man's will received a greater wound than his intellect in the Fall, according to Christian tradition. Nevertheless, there was a weakening of the intellect as a secondary consequence of original sin. It is this weakening of the intellect which Jaki sees as a type of "blindness" to reality, and which was responsible for the stillbirths of science. Thus he notes the nuance in the teaching of Vatican I about the possibility of a rational proof of the existence of God: "Whatever the full reasonability of the classic proofs of the existence of God, moral help in the form of salvation through revelation was needed for their steadfast espousal."[39]

As regards the wound to the will, Jaki frequently shows how this can be seen in the technological abuse of the products of science: "Disbelief in original sin did not remedy the obvious impotence of scientists as well as non-scientists to put an end to a course of action that could appear far more effective in hastening the advent of doomsday than all the angelic trumpets taken together."[40] Science was born from a Christian matrix. However, during the Renaissance and afterwards, this same science and its applications became distanced from the Christian culture which had given it birth in the first place. The price paid for this autonomy of science is that the products of technology are not referred back, for their rightful use, to that matrix which also embodies the Christian system of moral discernment. The salvation of man and the healing of his intellect and will was to be achieved by Christ the Saviour. We now turn to the manner in which the Christian doctrine of Creation has been given a distinct character by the dogma of the Incarnation.

That in Jaki's perception strong links exist between the dogmas of Creation and Incarnation has already been hinted at. He in fact shows in detail how the development of the doctrine of *creatio ex nihilo* was "connected with the conceptual refinements of the doctrine of Incarnation around which raged the great inner debates of the early Church."[41]

Jaki discusses the changes undergone by Jewish thought on creation during the first few centuries of Christianity. He, of course, begins with Philo, a contemporary of Jesus, and the subject of widely divergent interpretations. Jaki takes the view that Philo, who paid special attention to the meaning of Genesis 1, stands closer to "Greek eternalism than to Biblical creationism." The biblical view of creation, as Jaki argues, was much more apparent in the Book of Enoch, the Book of Jubilees, and in Fourth Esdras, all composed during the first century. Future trends were, however, more along the line set by Philo than by the apocalyptic literature. Within a few centuries, the earliest midrashim (called Bereshit Rabbi) "showed that Jewish theologians were no longer willing to uphold the doctrine of the complete submission of matter to the Maker of all."[42] In Jaki's tracing of this development, special attention is given to medieval Jewish cabbalistic lore. The heavy presence in it of obscurantist mysticism, invited, in the long run, open flirtation with emanationism. This further strenghtened the contrast between Christian eagerness to defend *creatio ex nihilo* and a sort of resignation within Judaism in regard to pantheism.

Jaki sees a partial explanation of this contrast in the effort of Judaism to oppose Christianity, evident especially in its rejection, towards the end of the first century, of the Alexandrian list of Old Testament books, a list which had already been espoused by Christians. This list included all the deuterocanonical books, among which are the Book of Wisdom and the Second Book of Maccabees, both of which, as we have seen, are important for the development of the dogma of creation. In the Islamic religion too there was a tendency in the Mutazalite tradition to slide towards emanationism and pantheism which led, in the case of Avicenna and Averroes, to plain endorsement of the pantheistic necessitarianism of Aristotle.

Jaki repeatedly asserts, and with distinct originality, that in Christianity a slide into pantheism was prevented because the doctrine of the creation was bolstered by faith in the Incarnation. Pantheism is invariably present when the eternal and cyclic view of the cosmos prevails. Belief in the uniqueness of the Incarnation and Redemption forestalled any cavorting with eternalist and cyclic world views. The uniqueness of Christ imposes a linear view of history and makes Christianity more than just one among many historical factors influencing the world. Or to quote Jaki, the dogmas of Creation and Incarnation mean "an absolute and most revolutionary break with a past steeped in paganism." He also warns that full implementation of the impact to be made by these dogmas is "an uphill fight never to be completed."[43]

It is well worth reflecting on Jaki's insistence, not to be found elsewhere, on the dogma about Christ as the only begotten (*monogenēs, unigenitus*) of the Father, as the very factor that prevented the sliding of Christianity into pantheism. Jaki does more than recall the fact that with the Greeks and Romans, the expression *monogenēs* or *unigenitus* "had the universe for its supreme reference point."[44] He further argues that belief in Christ as *monogenēs* put "a damper on any flirtation with the idea that any other being might be a divine begetting in terms of an emanationism which always carries an animist touch."[45] In the Christian vision, he argues, "the exaltedness of the universe remained intact as it was lowered through that infinite distance which is between Creator and creature."[46]

Further, he shows, again with a distinct touch of originality, that the dogma of Incarnation can be undermined by a faulty view of creation, a process of which the converse has so far been discussed. It is in this light that Jaki discusses the Arian controversy, in particular Arius whose "primary and real error resided in his concept of creation and Creator,"[47] a concept based on a neo-Platonist emanationism. Such an emanationism, which reduced the transcendence of God by making the world almost divine, obviated the need for any real Incarnation. Against Arius, it was necessary to affirm, first of all, the equality of the Son with the Father via the expression *homoousios*. Inferences to creation were not, however, long in coming. As Jaki shows with a remarkably novel analysis of Athanasius' anti-Arian writings, the idea of a fully divine Logos implied that his creative work was the "the paragon of logic and order." The rationality of the cosmos is thus "rooted in belief in the strict divinity of the Logos."[48]

Christ's coming also safeguards the right notion of purpose in man and in the universe. In particular, Jaki shows with great originality how the fact of Incarnation presupposes the existence of an immortal human soul, excludes every compromise with materialism, and assures eternal purpose for the individual. He recalls Jesus' answer to the good thief, "Today you will be with me in Paradise" (Lk 23:43) and His descent among the dead (part of the Creed) as incisive, though much neglected, tokens of the continuity of Christ's living human soul between his death and resurrection. This continuity can, however, be guaranteed only if Christ possessed an immortal human soul. Thus the connection between Creation and Incarnation has a direct impact on Christian anthropology. In Jaki's words, "Creator,

God Incarnate, creation out of nothing, immortal soul, and human dignity are notions that form a closely knit unit, a fact well attested by the story of the dogma of creation."[49] Man as the apex of the divinely created cosmos forms the subject-matter of the next chapter.

5

Man's Cosmos

Man is simultaneously a material object, a living being, a focus of mental activities.

Alexis Carrel, *Man the Unknown*

The adequate view of man

The dogma of the Incarnation, as has been seen in the previous chapter, sheds new light on man as part of creation, for, as Jaki states: "Christ's very being contradicts any doubt about man's being radically different from the rest of creation and even from the rest of the evolutionary process."[1] It has already been noted that Jaki regards the universe as a highly specific entity, ordained, in all evidence, for the creation of man, an inference not incompatible with the phrase, "anthropic principle," frequently used in modern cosmological literature.[2] He warns that contrary to its prevalent interpretation, that principle can only mean that the right conditions were present for the creation of man, which is something very different from the view that man is a necessary outcome of the primordial "cosmic soup." He further insists that the position of scientific man in the cosmos indicates something of his very own nature: Man is both part of the cosmos and yet vastly superior to it. Since man has a precise and sophisticated grasp of the cosmos he cannot be a mere beast

66

"whose universe is limited to the surroundings available to its sensory organs."[3] Finally, Jaki claims that the specificity of the universe, which is revealed through man's laborious scientific work should discourage the view that man acquires his knowledge of the universe in the angelic manner implicitly advocated by Descartes and the rationalist tradition. The interaction between mind and body is not mechanical, as is seen from the fact that man makes errors in doing science.

An epistemological balance between empiricism and rationalism or materialism and idealism is a goal often advocated by Jaki. He finds that balance embodied in a middle road between the monistic (materialist and idealist) conceptions of man as a mere beast or as pure spirit. The balance implies, according to him, a dualism in which the soul is to be conceived neither as a ghost in a machine nor as a mere epiphenomenon of the brain. Jaki considers that the expression "rational animal"[4] suitably describes a middle road in the description of the nature of man. He finds that the moderate realism to be followed in epistemology not only corresponds to a balanced view of man but also forms the basis of scientific work as well as of natural theology. A rational approach to God through visible creation is blocked if the mind is but a machine; nor is that approach needed if the mind "is a disembodied spirit, trapped in the body." To continue with Jaki, "both science and natural theology demand a view of the mind in which justice is done both to the mind's essential dependence on the body and to the mind's ability to reach not only beyond its own body but also beyond the totality of bodies or the universe."[5]

Jaki draws out some subtleties of man's relationship with the cosmos. Since man is part of material creation "he cannot take up a post beyond the universe, so as to overlook it as though he were its conqueror." Nevertheless man's scientific conquest of the cosmos is a function of man's very nature, which therefore must transcend the realm of the sensory. Jaki powerfully illustrates this superiority of man over the cosmos: "Unless one is sensitive enough to marvel at the ability of man to think, no conviction will be carried by the contrast between man, who knows that a mere drop of water can extinguish him, and the whole universe which knows nothing of its ability, or of the ability of even its smallest part, to crush man in a split second."[6]

The time dependence of the cosmos as perceived by man prompts on Jaki's part various observations reminiscent of Pascal: Both man and the cosmos are limited by time, but the essential difference between man and the cosmos is that man notices and reflects upon this time-dependence. Thus while man is restricted by time, he also transcends it: "while the universe knows nothing of its transitoriness, man is able to perceive not only his own transitoriness but also that of the universe. . . . It has been through the specificity of cosmic time that man has obtained his deepest insight into the enormously specific structure of the universe."[7]

Jaki describes the right order between the view of the true nature of man and of the scientific endeavour insofar as guaranteed by faith in God the Creator: "Only with God in view will man be protected from ending up either as a fallen angel or a glorified ape and will his confidence, his most cherished possession, be protected from being sapped by his spectacular conquests, which ought to be so many proofs that he is unconquerable."[8] Jaki's view of the true nature of man is further made clear by his rejection of several inadequate views of man. These are, as he shows, often coupled with an epistemological imbalance which can but cause difficulties in the recognition of God the Creator.

Some inadequate views of man

Jaki's survey of mistaken visions of man's nature is related to the scientific enterprise and therefore begins with Descartes. The latter started the trend which over-emphasized the rational part of man, at the expense of his material body. Connected with this is the fact, to quote Jaki, that "he was the first of modern scientists who fell to the temptation in which man is lured into deriving a priori the shape, structure, and laws of the universe." This apriorism brought with it the view that the world was necessary, a notion which could only weaken the theological notion of God. In Jaki's words, "a God who is bound by inner necessity to create the very world which exists is a poor shadow of himself."[9]

Jaki finds the root of Descartes' apriorism and his failure in physical science in his mistaken view that man is a "ghost in a machine."[10] In line with his emphasis on extension, Descartes subjected the soul to spatiality, as he located it in the pineal gland. In

Descartes' attempt to eliminate the mystery from the mind-body relationship, Jaki notes a Copernican revolution in reverse. Copernicus turned "geocentrism into heliocentrism, and let heliocentrism rest on theocentrism, the best, even the only safeguard against anthropocentrism of any kind." Descartes, on the other hand, locked human thought "into an anthropocentrism which could serve only as a strait-jacket for science."[11] Moreover, in Descartes' universe, God was only required to perform a primordial act which was far less than a creation out of nothing.

Jaki states that Descartes' anthropocentrism influenced several generations of thinkers and that Western philosophy has suffered ever since from a repetitive pattern of transient systems, such as idealism, positivism, and existentialism. Once the healthy balance of moderate realism had been abandoned, lop-sidedness had to characterize scientifically articulated views of the mind-body relationship. The latter, in Jaki's words, "is a mysterious coin, with two luminous sides. The only way to handle it is to follow the advice once given about a tax coin and render both mind and body their respective dues." While Saint Thomas emphasized simultaneously the priority of the sensory realm and the active role of the intellect, both emphases, to quote Jaki, "could but degenerate into shibboleths of empiricism and idealism once they were no longer considered as two sides of one and the same coin."[12]

A chief figure in the process was, according to Jaki, Kant and precisely because of his self-delusion of doing philosophy in a "scientific" way. Such a way was but a mask for Kant's ulterior and pseudo-religious aim of establishing man as an autonomous being. He failed to see that criticism presupposes knowledge, nor did he perceive that he invited "sheer subjectivism, nay solipsism, which cuts one off from the rest of the universe." In the *Critique of Pure Reason* Kant used the so-called critical principle to establish the claim that "universe, soul, and God — the three main objects of metaphysics — were but the bastard products of the cravings of the human intellect." In the *Opus postumum*, as Jaki pointedly recalls, Kant spells out the ultimate pseudo-religious aspect of that subjectivism: "God is not a being outside me but merely a thought within me."[13]

Kant's epistemology was based on his highly imbalanced view of man in which man is mostly a mind; this made natural theology impossible. Science was also threatened by the same imbalance.

Having exalted the intellect at the expense of the sensory realm, Kant discredited the a posteriori way of acquiring knowledge. Through his apriorism Kant, whom Jaki regards as the modern Procrustes, was led to tailor the universe to man's ordinary perception, which included a "naive and stubborn espousal of the infinite Euclidean universe with its homogeneous distribution of stars." The death-knell for Kant's apriorism and indeed his whole system was soon to come from scientific corners, a point which Jaki emphasizes with great originality. He recalls that already Helmholtz had taken the view that the formulation of non-Euclidean geometries had undercut Kant's epistemology. With an eye on the fact that General Relativity had secured the scientific notion of the cosmos, Jaki notes that a major blow has been thereby dealt to Kant's metaphysics. In Jaki's words, "the mind can do much more than Kant imagined." Among such deeds of science are, in Jaki's view, Gödel's theorems of incompleteness that put a damper on a priori conceptualizations of the universe. Jaki insists that ideas and facts must be considered together, for they "constitute a pair," forming a "coherence within which they retain their distinctness."[14]

Fichte, Schelling and Hegel are Jaki's next illustration of the same lesson of abusing science in support of a mistaken epistemology. In Jaki's words, Hegel took man for mind and wanted nature to be understood through the "interiorization of the mind." In this idealistic Naturphilosophie, no room was left for experimental science. This Jaki illustrates with many quotations from Hegel, among them the one conveying his aim "to convey an image of nature, in order to subdue this Proteus: to find in this externality only the mirror of ourselves, to see in nature a free reflection of spirit: to understand God, not in the contemplation of spirit, but in this His immediate essence."[15] Hegelian idealism left the mind incapable of making distinctions between the living and the non-living, between spirit and matter and between being and non-being. Further, Jaki points out that the Hegelian view of man and reality had disastrous consequences for humanity: Hegel's system generated a Right and a Left which "achieved their maddening distinction through the numbers of cruel deaths they produced."[16] That man became a "fallen angel" was to be clearly seen in the diabolical systems of Nazi Germany, Leninist and Stalinist Russia, and Maoist China.

Man as pure matter is the theme of three "scientific" tendencies discussed in detail by Jaki. The first is the attempt of the evolutionists to reduce man to a mere animal. The second is the attempt to elevate the inanimate computer to the level of man who made it; this is effectively to reduce man again to the purely material. In the third, which transpires in fashionable views on extra-terrestrial intelligence, man appears as a chance product of blind forces. All three trends reveal a thrust that aims at promoting materialist views of man.

As to the view of man endorsed by "evolutionists," Jaki places its beginning in the writings of Descartes and Rousseau who, for all their differences, obeyed a similar logic: "Descartes seized on the mind and boosted man into an angel. Rousseau took the sentiments, but having no eyes for the head, he aimed at the heart and hit the target somewhat lower, where the beast loves to reside in man."[17] With Rousseau, who claimed man to be autonomous with respect to duty and moral law, man became a function of his sentiments and longings. It was no surprise, Jaki notes, that Rousseau glorified the ape in man. In a world governed by instincts there remained little room for "stability, order and logic." Jaki illustrates these connections with a quotation from Rousseau: "All on earth is a continual flux which does not allow anything to take on a constant form."[18] Not unexpectedly, Jaki, who argues against Rousseau with reference to the basic assumption of science that the world is rational, coherent and capable of investigation, further exposes Rousseau by quoting his description of all sciences "as born out of vice and having evil for their object."[19]

Jaki insists that Darwin inherited the train of thought begun by Rousseau. Paradoxical as it may seem, Rousseau, who was against the sciences, "set for the science of man a new course," by bequeathing to posterity a romanticist denial of basic distinctions which, so Jaki argues, Darwin capped with rank materialism. In proof of this Jaki quotes from Darwin's early notebooks which contain, among them, the phrase: "Why is thought, being a secretion of the brain, more wonderful than gravity, a property of matter?" Having deprived man of the spiritual side of his nature, Darwin's norm became an allegiance to the absence of all norms. In Jaki's words, this system "beckoned toward unfathomable whirls in which one was no more than flotsam hurled round and round by the blindest of blind fates."[20]

It is necessary, so Jaki warns, for the Christian to distinguish the "gold from the straw in the evolutionary theory." Time has a special dignity within the framework of Christian faith, because Christ came in time. Hence the attempt to understand the biological realm in its time–development should pose no problem. Yet Jaki notes that some modern Christian thinkers have failed to notice the "huge piles of straw" in evolutionary theory. This failure of theirs lies in not noticing that the Darwinian theory effectively turns time into a hopeless treadmill. Nor did Darwin notice that Christian faith liberated man from a pessimistic imprisonment within a world–picture based on inexorable cycles in time. It is rather tragic, Jaki notes, that, having been freed from the bondage of ancient pagan visions, man should once again fall prey to the cyclic world view. As an illustration Jaki recalls T. H. Huxley's endorsement of "the vision of a meaningless evolution in which higher and lower were indistinguishable precisely because moving into the future was not, in the Darwinian perspective, different from receding into the past." The confrontation with Darwinism once again brought to the fore the relation between human nature and time within Christian theology, as had already been seen in the great clash involving "nascent Christianity and Hellenistic culture over the question whether life, including the redeeming life of Christ, was a once-and-for-all proposition, or whether life was mere flotsam on the unfathomable cyclic currents of blind cosmic force."[21]

Jaki points out in the same context that there is no opposition between creation and evolution, but he takes care lest his words be taken for an endorsement, however indirect, of creationism. He insists, however, that the clash of Christians with Darwinism (as not co-terminous with evolutionary perspective) arises because the latter is a materialist position incompatible with creation. Further, according to Jaki, the basic problem in the Darwinian perspective on evolution is its blindness towards purpose and mind in a philosophy of "ultimate meaninglessness, in which the partial aspects are found meaningful, but never the whole." Jaki notes that Darwinism finds its most fertile growth on Anglo-Saxon soil: there "the encyclopaedias contain articles on evolution, anthropology, family, procreation, education, psychology, language, and even on intelligence, while Man as such is ignored."[22]

According to Jaki, the blunder of those who regard man as essentially on the same level as the rest of creation lies in anthropomorphism which presents "nature as a personality with striving" and depicts a cosmic process which "gains consciousness and begins to comprehend itself." Man then becomes but a phase in a cosmos which is gradually acquiring a pseudo-personhood. This conception "flies in the face of that very resolve that helped science rise four hundred years ago."[23] It also undermines the Christian vision of man in a world created by God. Jaki accepts evolution as the "factual though still very imperfectly understood instrumentality of a species in the rise of another," and he adds that "the incompleteness of understanding is even greater concerning the rise of genera, and grows exponentially as the emergence of even more encompassing units — classes, orders, and phyla — is considered."[24] Jaki also relates the Darwinian approach with attempts to see the great advances in physics as explaining completely the nature and function of living organisms. Jaki makes it clear that there is an interplay between physics and biology,[25] while warning that random chance is incapable of being the basis of the study of living organisms.

The most fundamental point made by Jaki as regards the reductionism of Darwinist approaches to anthropology is that the dogma of the Incarnation guarantees the true nature of man. The tenet that Christ had an immortal human soul is key in this respect, for "it is upon that soul, inseparably united to his divine nature and divine person, that Scripture and the Creeds predicate Christ's descent into hell." Belief in Christ's human soul reinforces the fact that man is "radically different from the rest of creation and even from the rest of the evolutionary process."[26]

The reduction of man to sheer biology has its reverse in claims about the possibility of "artificial intelligence," the second aspect of Jaki's concern for threats to Christian anthropology that ultimately strike at the Christian doctrine of creation. He shows the fallacy of those claims by reviewing their alleged supports in computer technology, brain research, psychology, and philosophy. He extensively documents his thesis that from Pascal to Von Neumann and beyond, "all great contributors to the theory and development of computers refused to attribute thinking or consciousness to them."[27] A chief reason behind that refusal is the recognition that the computer is limited by the physicial features of its components. In Jaki's words, "physics has its built-in limitations that cannot be overcome by its products, however marvelous."[28] His argumentation is well summed up in his quoting a statement about the ENIAC (electronic numerical integrator and calculator) made in the 1940's at the University of Pennsylvania. This machine could "only do precisely what it is told to do; the decisions on what to tell it to do, and the thought which lies behind these decisions, have to be taken by those who are operating it. Use of the machine is no substitute for the thought of organizing the computations, only for the labour of carrying them out."[29]

Concerning the bearing of biology and brain research on the merits of artificial intelligence, Jaki's argument may be summed up as follows. There is a large gap between the living and non-living, but the separation between the rational and the purely biological is incomparably greater. Since the physicalists have so far been unable to explain the former difference, the burden of proof that the human brain is but a computer rests with the physicalist, not with the dualist. Jaki makes much of the failure of the physicalists to identify "memory units, memory storing and memory retrieval processes in the brain."[30] Some of the parts of the brain "may act as a thermostat, a radar, or a computer but it far transcends even the most advanced form of such mechanisms."[31]

That the brain cannot be reduced to a computer can also be seen from the psychological viewpoint, which is Jaki's third main point on artificial intelligence. Although eighteenth- and nineteenth-century associationist psychologists modelled their speculations on physics, "Fechner, most of the early associationists, and Locke, were still dualists."[32] Jaki finds in Freud the one who grafted physicalism onto psychology by proposing one basic kind of energy (libido). All other psychic energies were for Freud "the more or less overt manifestations of man's sexual drive."[33] Concerning the ensuing debate between various schools of psychology (such as the psychoanalyst followers of Freud, the Jungians, and the behaviourists), Jaki claims that their differences often lay in the "measure of carrying physics into psychology,"[34] and not in their resolve to endorse and promote reductionism.

The intricacy of consciousness as revealed by modern psychology indicates for Jaki that the human psyche is far too rich a reality to be reduced to a computer. Man is at once "a perceiving, thinking and feeling agent,"[35] a living organic unity, to which physicalist psychology is unable to do justice. Jaki also shows the link among three intellectual trends of this century: operationism in physics, behaviorism in psychology, and logical positivism in philosophy. Their common aim is to undermine "absolute concepts in physics, dualistic mentality in psychology, and rational metaphysics."[36]

Jaki's fourth perspective on artificial intelligence concerns its philosophical presuppositions. He shows that language itself and its written symbolism are an indication of the fallacy of physicalism. He states that "we know about thoughts and concepts only through spoken and written words, but it is also well known that concepts are not strictly codified in words." The fact that thoughts and concepts transcend language points to a human mind whose functions transcend the operation of a mere machine. Jaki finds it most significant that Wittgenstein failed to build up a mechanical system of language from atomistic concepts.[37] The theological background of language is also set forth by Jaki, who shows that belief in Christ implies a profound respect for language and that the very opposite sets the tone of endorsements of artificial intelligence: "Belief in the Word (Logos), eternally uttered by the Father, has become the salvation of human words as well. Only in that perspective have those words remained immune to being degraded into mere tools of facile intellectual games, all aimed at undermining the intellect itself."[38] Such a threat is posed, according to Jaki, by the abolition, demanded by the ideology of artificial intelligence, of the difference between behavior and experience: "while behavior is essentially to perform something, to do something, subjective experience is not a derivative of one's externally observed performance or behavior."[39] While a human person exhibits behaviour and has experience, a computer can at most behave as if it had experience. An act of experience cannot logically be built into a machine.

In Jaki's view, an important argument against artificial intelligence can be derived from Gödel's incompleteness theorems, according to which it is impossible to prove the consistency of a given system of arithmetical propositions from the system itself. Yet the truth of those theorems can only be maintained if one grants the immediacy with which human reasoning assures itself, on its own grounds, about its own rationality. A machine, being a purely formal system, cannot have such assurance about itself and, therefore, cannot be its own starting point.

Jaki offers carefully nuanced views on how one should proceed in opposing false notions concerning artificial intelligence. He makes it clear that speculations on thinking machines derive strong support from Darwinians who maintain a strict continuity between mind and matter. Jaki insists that computers do not have wisdom, creativity, understanding, intelligence, nor do they have the ability to make discoveries. In his words, "the computer no more discovers anything than does a slide rule or an abacus." However, Jaki warns that inadequacies in computer programming and technology cannot form a basis of demonstrating Christian dualism: "Such a basis would prove as counterproductive as did those arguments in which shortcomings of physical science were taken for a justification to invoke God. Holes in scientific knowledge have an uncanny way of being filled up and leave shortsighted divines stranded."[40]

The key to dealing with the false philosophies tied to the notion of artificial intelligence is moderate or methodical realism. Jaki grounds this realism philosophically in the fact that the human "mind operates in and through a body." On the theological level, moderate realism "owes its allegiance to dogmatically defined tenets about Christ as a union of two natures (divine and human) in one divine person."[41] Thus the believer in an Incarnate God must hold the soul to be immortal and divinely created and to be united only with matter insofar as it forms a human body. Jaki also points out that the concept of thinking machines poses a threat to consistency in thinking about the laws of nature, a threat which he also notes in reference to speculations about extra-terrestrial intelligence.

The laws of nature which Jaki investigated in great detail in that latter respect relate to the formation of planetary systems. He in fact produced the most complete history of theories of the origin of planetary systems, which was hailed as "a truly exceptional work."[42] In proof of the theologian he is when he writes on the history of physics, he brought to the surface the impact which infatuation with planetarians, or the principle of plenitude,[43] had on the formation of those theories. He shows with the great erudition of a leading historian of astronomy, that beneath theories (invariably unsatisfactory) that imply the presence of planetary systems around most stars, there always lay the desire to see intelligent beings in every corner of the universe. As Jaki shows, such a multiplication of intelligent beings is an invariable offshoot of the assumption that human intelligence is an automatic outcome of physico-chemical diversification. He shows that assumption to be at work in Kant's cosmogonical work, the Third Part of which he was the first to make available to the English reader.[44]

Jaki makes much of the fact that science has shown the earth to be an extremely fine-tuned life-support mechanism. The physical characteristics of the earth which "set narrow limits to the evolution of life on it, are in turn the function of its density, chemical composition, distance from the sun, and of the mass and size of the sun." The balance is so delicate that "if the mass of Jupiter were to be increased by one percent, the planetary system would no longer have that stability which is a precondition of life on earth." On the other hand, there remains the possibility of life on other planets. The solar system may not be unique. As Jaki warns: "Nothing is more self-defeating in matters scientific than to declare that persistent failure to discover or to explain something means that it will remain forever beyond our grasp, intellectual or observational. The entire history of science is a witness to the truth of the principle that the unknown of yesterday becomes the novelty of today and the commonplace of tomorrow."[45]

What Jaki writes about more recent speculations on ETI (extraterrestrial intelligence) shows again his bent to connect his studies as a historian of science with his theological interest. On the one hand he argues (and here one finds a telling aspect of the ties he builds between creation and scientific creativity) that interest in ETI has not promoted the progress of astronomy.[46] On the other hand he shows that infatuation with ETI has always sought support in the materialist ideology of Darwinism which presents man as chance product of purely material forces. In Jaki's words, "fashionable speculations on ETI, nay brave assertions of its factuality, are so many rigged testimonials in a courtroom set up to banish God from the realm of the living, to pre-empt purpose of all its significance, and to assure the rule of meaninglessness."[47]

Whatever Jaki's scorn for efforts at detecting radio signals from outer space, he keeps an open mind about the possibility of ETI, though for reasons that are not centered on science. Holding that science can at best beg the question of ETI, he turns to philosophy and theology. The possibility of a rational discourse between ETI and human beings presupposes, according to him, a universality of the intellect which can be argued only on the basis of metaphysical realism. This is, however, precisely the perspective that can have no place within Darwinism, or in general, "within a philosophical discourse which rests, directly or indirectly, on nominalism." As to theology, his reflections are summed up in his statement: "No one can prescribe to God to create intellects everywhere or to limit his power to do so."[48]

In his rejection of the reductionist views of man, Jaki has defended the existence of the human soul as a created entity. He has shown that as soon as one casts doubt on the true nature of man, one closes the road to the recognition of God the Creator. He has also offered insightful reflections, based on the history of science, on the consequences which a materialist view of man has for social and political life, our next topic.

Man and ethics

In Jaki's view, the construction of ethics depends on an understanding of the nature of man. The nature of man stood in the center of "philosophical debates that led to Ockham's nominalism, and beyond it to empiricism and rationalism."[49] The debate turned especially around the question whether there was a human nature shared by all men. Nominalism gave heavy support to the view that there are only individuals. In the long run nominalism encouraged scepticism about universally valid ethical values and invited world views based on randomness. The Darwinian view of man and Darwinian ethics were inevitable consequences.

Jaki emphasizes two points in thinking about man as preliminary to a sound system of ethics. First, it is necessary to view man as a body and soul in unity as traditionally taught in Christian doctrine: "A reacceptance of dualism by secular society is the only road toward social health."[50] Second, the christological foundation of this dualism must be seen in bold relief. As has already been noted, Jaki makes much of that point of christology which posits an immortal human soul in Christ as the safeguard of his human identity between his death and resurrection. Jaki emphasizes no less the notion that belief in our own immortal soul is equally the logical ground for our belief in our bodily resurrection. With these two ideas in mind he feels entitled to conclude: "No wonder that from reason's probing into the mystery of the Incarnation there also derived a view of man as a person with inalienable dignity."[51]

Apart from these dogmatic foundations of ethics, ultimately rooted in the Christian doctrine of creation, Jaki does not fail to emphasize that ethical values are not derivable from science itself. Such grounds of ethics as the freedom of man's will and the purposefulness of human existence are as much outside the competence of science as is the ultimate explanation of the cosmos. In Jaki's words, "an ethical science can only be such which takes its ethical norms from an ethics existing independently of science." Such an ethics gradually vanished from view once "Western philosophy had abandoned Christian vistas,"[52] with a consequent rift between means and purpose.

According to Jaki, a principal step in the process was Kant's opting for subjectivism, which, through the Hegelian Left fomented the moral arbitrariness of communism. The latter found, of course, much use for its purposes in Darwinist perspectives: "The enthusiasm for Darwinism of the advocates of the dictatorship of the proletariat and of a master race is all too understandable. Marx was quick to notice the usefulness of Darwinist theory for promoting class struggle, and Hitler volubly echoed Darwinist views very popular among German military leaders prior to the First World War as a justification of their and his plans."[53] Modern Western democracies rest, according to Jaki, on grounds far less secure than usually assumed and for reasons very similar to the ones just outlined: "The real enemies of open society are not societies based on absolute and even on supernatural revealed truths, but the ideas of intellectual circles that opted for chance as the ultimate. . . . Ideas are more dangerous than weapons." Western society is living on borrowed capital, which consists in the effectiveness of long abandoned beliefs in absolute norms. Since Christian revelation, the matrix of those norms and background of those beliefs, is no longer acknowledged, secular society has turned, in Jaki's strong word, into a mere "parasite."[54]

Jaki calls attention to existentialism as a further factor in the disintegration of absolute ethical values. According to him, Sartre's existentialism "does away with all norms, all restrictions, and also with all continuity."[55] Since in Sartre's system only the discrete moments, absolutely isolated from each other, are relevant, time can no longer provide that continuum which is the parameter of enduring moral law and responsibility. Jaki also shows that philosophies (such as that of Kuhn), which aim at describing society and science in terms of revolutions, undermine both science and society through their incoherence: "At stake is the very health of society in which many are swept up in a merry march toward an anarchical state of affairs."[56]

The category of "should" may be considered by modern man "as an old-fashioned prison, yet within its walls he shall forever remain. These walls shall not disappear by a policy which professes them to be non-existent."[57] In fact, at no time in history have ethics been more needed than today, for scientific discoveries raise many questions for a society weak in moral resolve. As Jaki graphically states: "Scientists leave their discoveries, like foundlings, on the doorstep of society, while the step-parents do not know how to bring them up."[58] The fact remains that both ethics and science require a coherence in space and time, which can be maintained only in the framework of moderate realism. Science is developing on the strength of values which it has inherited; yet today there is no accompanying Christian cultural matrix to prevent its products being used for ill, and to encourage the constructive use of them.

In the moral disorientation of modern man, Jaki sees a major manifestation of original sin in which, as was already noted, he finds the indispensable background for the understanding of the impact which christological doctrines made on the scientific enterprise. He is not afraid to see sin for what it is, and to call for a cure for it in revelation and grace rather than temporary panaceas. In support of this, he quotes Albert Einstein, who stated in the face of atomic destruction that "the real problem is in the minds and hearts of men."[59] He also recalls a contrast drawn by General Omar Bradley: "We have grasped the mystery of the atom and we rejected the Sermon on the Mount. Ours is a world of nuclear giants and ethical infants."[60] Among the issues which Jaki raises about a "scientific" ethics are the ones related to genetic engineering, such as "whether to permit the creation of humans in test tubes; or to permit or not to permit the chemical refashioning of brain processes; or to permit or not to permit the interference with one's genetic stock."[61]

Jaki highlights the spread of the moral disease of abortion by referring to the "scientifically" verifiable fact that "in some states abortions are already outnumbering live births."[62] He sees an abuse of science in the absurdity of the arms race   as well as in some modern business trends. He points out problems that arise whenever in a world of finance, which is fuelled by the ever new products of science and technology, there remains no ethical consensus. About all such problems Jaki holds high the view: "History clearly shows that it was only a Western world steeped in Christianity that was capable of creating science, economy, and business on a scale never witnessed before. This capability was a will to decide about a course of action which was deemed to be in consonance with man's position in nature as its God-appointed steward. To carry on with this course of action man needed a will corrected and strengthened by a transcendental vision which no philosophy or worldly wisdom could provide. It was only within a Christian matrix that man was able to live up to his capability of making decisions, which is the exclusive capability of an ethical animal."[63]

This chapter brings to a close the basic part of this work, in which we first considered Jaki's views on the nature of science and its relation, historical and philosophical, to the Christian creed from which it developed. Jaki's views on the Christian belief in God the Creator, as the primary object of that creed, and on man, the very subject of that faith, were finally seen in their extension to the grounds of an ethics for science at this actual, crucial stage of history. It will be the task of the remaining chapters to appraise his views vis-à-vis its evaluation by his peers and especially against the background of the numerous utterances of the actual magisterial voice of the Church concerning science and creation.

6

Jaki and his Critics

I am nothing if not critical
Shakespeare, *Othello*

Fair criticism should begin by saying first what the author meant to say. Second, the critic should consider the terms or the framework chosen by the author to present his thesis. The critic's task is particularly taxing when he is faced with a wide variety of theses proposed by an author as is the case with Jaki's works. Fortunately, Jaki's statements on Christian belief in God the Creator are often pivoted on two great discoveries of intellectual history which, in a subtle sense, he was the first to recognize as such. One of them is the discovery of science itself, or its only viable birth in the Middle Ages, as set against the stillbirths of science in all great ancient cultures, that is, the failure of those cultures to discover science. The other is the scientific discovery of the universe in terms of the cosmology of General Relativity and of its experimental consequences, above all the discovery of the 2.7°K background radiation in 1965.

The foregoing chapters offered various details on these two discoveries in terms of Jaki's reflections that are governed by his endorsement of an ancient aphorism as rephrased by Lord Boling-brooke: "History is philosophy teaching by examples."[1] Therefore his very reflections could but put further emphasis on the importance of those two discoveries that impose a profound reappraisal of the history of science and of the philosophical understanding of the universe. Critics, who mostly present themselves as reviewers of books, certainly expose themselves to criticism when they pay but slight attention to towering points in an author's work or when they give them a slant that cannot be found in his writings, let alone when they say nothing of those very points.

The discovery about history

One way of demonstrating the reliability of historical data is to show that an author is not alone in using them. Jaki is, of course, most emphatic in acknowledging his debt to Duhem as the one who made a breakthrough in the historiography of science by his unveiling the true birth of science in the Middle Ages.[2] As regards ancient cultures, Duhem only considered ancient Greece. Jaki is the first to consider systematically the stillbirth of science in all major ancient cultures. Jaki's detailed discussion of the topic stands in sharp contrast to A. N. Whitehead's brief, though often recalled remarks on the contribution of medieval scholasticism to the unique birth of science in Europe.[3] Also, whereas for Whitehead Christian faith promoted that birth unconsciously, Jaki regards the process as being "most conscious."[4] Again, as is not the case with Jaki's arguments, the theological perspective is rather weak in the writings of various scholars who traced the birth of modern science to a radical break with Aristotle's dynamics. Instances of this are F. Copleston's reference to the continuity from Philoponus to the impetus theory of Buridan and Oresme[5] and E. J. Dijksterhuis' extensive discussion of the same topic.[6] A. C. Crombie also regards the Middle Ages as important for the rise of science without putting sufficient emphasis on the theological factor.[7]

A growing awareness among Protestant scholars about a strong connection between the rise of science and the Christian theology of creation is largely due to articles written in the mid-1930s by M. B. Foster, a tutor at Christ Church, Oxford.[8] One would, however, look in vain in those articles for an appreciation of Duhem's massive studies and of medieval scholasticism, which Foster takes for a continuation of Aristotelian necessitarianism. L. Gilkey, basing himself on Foster's work, stressed the importance of the Christian origins of modern science, but failed to note the historical context, the Middle Ages.[9] Similar oversight of the medieval matrix was shown by G. B. Deason as he argued that a specifically Protestant Christianity was the causal factor in the rise of science and listed a number of authors who held this position either strongly or weakly.[10] It was by ignoring the medieval centuries that R. Hooykaas traced thematically the rise of science to the theology of the Reformation.[11] D. M. Mackay, another Protestant supporter of that view, had but scornful remarks for the medieval tradition[12] as he ignored Duhem's monumental work altogether. E. Klaaren is a Protestant scholar who, in tracing the origins of modern science, barely mentions Duhem while taking a non-ontological view of creation.[13] Duhem's importance was acknowledged by V. Monod[14] whose work Jaki regards as much more scholarly than the writings of other Protestant authors. In general, Jaki notes an "almost systematic oversight of Duhem and of the Middle Ages in books written during the last two or three decades by Protestant scholars on the rise of science and Christianity."[15]

Several authors, who do not take the view that Christianity was responsible for the rise of science, nevertheless use historical data similar to the ones utilized by Jaki, though on a much narrower scale. One such author is C. A. Ronan, who notes the scientific failure of ancient Egyptians, Babylonians, Mesopotamians, Meso-Americans, Hindus, Chinese, Greeks and Arabs. As regards the medieval development of science, Ronan recalls the work of Buridan and Oresme and concludes: "It is in the physical sciences that we see most clearly the emergence of modern science, which was to a great extent based on the enquiring attitudes of late medieval scholars."[16] In indirect support of those medievals, Ronan describes Giordano Bruno as "turbulent and arrogant" with an organismic view of the universe, a view "motivated by Hermetic magic, not by a desire to rationalize the entire natural world in an organic fashion."[17] Although he notes the historical occurrence of several stillbirths and one viable birth of science, Ronan does not mention Duhem or Jaki, but acknowledges a debt to Kuhn who did not discuss those stillbirths at all![18] In interpreting these historical phenomena, Ronan concludes that the growth of science resulted from many factors, including "freedom of speculation," the "aspiration to break the mould of existing orthodoxies," and the influence of Protestantism.[19]

The sheer wealth of sources given in Jaki's works dealing with the unique rise of science is a measure of his credibility as his use of them can readily be verified. For example, about a third of his Gifford Lectures, *The Road of Science and the Ways to God*, is a series of carefully documented notes. This fact prompted authors critical of Jaki to register the scholarly value of his researches. Thus F. R. Haig, who took exception to Jaki's polemical tone, stated: "Jaki's book is a massively documented, exhaustively researched study of the history of science and philosophy," and concluded: "Jaki has penned a book which invites refutation and clarification if anyone can master the scholarship to try it."[20] This means that any critic of Jaki's position automatically incurs the burden of proof in the debate, a burden hardly ever assumed because of its unusual weight.

In sum, the historical fact of several stillbirths and a unique viable birth of science is admitted, however briefly at times, by various authors, in writings from a Catholic, or a Protestant, or a non-religious standpoint. Several reviewers are in explicit agreement with Jaki's use of his sources. Reviewers who agree with Jaki's conclusions are also the ones who extol the quality of his scholarship.[21] Views about his conclusions have a broad spectrum. There are authors who expressed respect. K. Cauthen mentions Jaki as one of a series of scholars (M. B. Foster, L. Gilkey, E. L. Mascall, H. Butterfield, A. N. Whitehead, C. F. von Weizsäcker, and P. Duhem) who "have been increasingly stressing the thesis that the Christian vision of God and the world provided some of the essential ingredients underlying the emergence of modern science. The proponents of this view typically point to a ferment in the thought of the late Middle Ages which generated habits of mind peculiarly congenial to empirical enquiry." In accordance with Jaki, Cauthen notes the importance of the decision of 1277 for the rise of science and states that "it was the increasing impact of ideas derived from the Hebrew-Christian doctrine of creation that led to the demise of Aristotelian natural philosophy and to the establishment of modes of understanding culminating in the triumph of Newtonian science."[22]

T. F. Torrance described the difference between the thinking within Christian culture and non-Christian cultures, as he stated that it was the doctrine of the "freedom of the creation contingent upon the freedom of God which liberated Christian thought from the tyranny of the fate, necessity, and determinism which for the pagan mind was clamped down upon creaturely existence by the inexorably cyclic processes of a self-sufficient universe."[23] In making this statement, Torrance acknowledges Jaki's work *Science and Creation*. Nevertheless, Torrance's conception of contingency differs from that of Jaki. Torrance follows the Reformed tradition in stating that "nothing can be established about contingency except through divine revelation,"[24] while Jaki uses the philosophical argument from contingency as a way of demonstrating the existence of God.

L. Newbigin, another Protestant author, asks why there should not have been a self-sustaining scientific enterprise (despite great intellectual power) among the ancient Chinese, Indians, Egyptians, and Greeks, while in modern times science is very much self-sustaining. Newbigin adds: "It has been very plausibly argued that the decisive factor is to be found in the biblical vision of the world as both rational and contingent. For to put it briefly, if the world is not rational, science is not possible; if the world is not contingent, science is not necessary." Newbigin regards Jaki as responsible for this "plausible argument" in his two books, *Science and Creation* and *The Road of Science and the Ways to God*.[25]

Jaki has greatly inspired P. E. Hodgson, a Catholic nuclear physicist, to see the link between the unique viable birth of science in Western Europe and Christian faith in God the Creator. With a direct reference to Jaki's researches and arguments Hodgson stated that "during the critical centuries before the birth of science the collective mind of Europe was moulded by a system of beliefs that included just those special elements that are necessary for the birth and growth of science. There is thus a living organic continuity between the Christian revelation and modern science."[26] Furthermore, L. Bouyer, a Catholic theologian, has remarked that Jaki has shown with masterly precision that modern science could not have been born without the contribution which medieval theology made to the reasoned understanding of Judeao-Christian Revelation concerning God the Creator.[27]

The various reviews of Jaki's works reflect a great diversity of attention to the history of science. References to the history of science are few and far between in a particularly negative review which is also one of the longest and most unappreciative. Ironically enough, its author, K. J. Sharpe, ends with what amounts to a high, though rather roundabout acclaim of Jaki's scholarship. Sharpe, who is not a scientist, also borrows from others his observations about the history of science. The essential position Sharpe takes is, however, his own: "From a logical point of view, belief in the rationality of the cosmos does not derive from Christian belief."[28] Such a position fails to take into account the invariably incomplete rationality which the Greeks ascribed to the universe. Quite different is the portrayal of cosmic rationality in the works of Jaki who makes much of the witness of history.

As a patently liberal Protestant, who dismissed Jaki's concern for a rational demonstration of the existence of an immortal soul and of the validity of the cosmological argument, Sharpe could hardly show sympathy for Jaki's marshalling of historical data. At any rate, whatever the logical possibility of reaching the idea of the rationality of the cosmos with no reference to Christian revelation, Jaki recently showed that the first factual statement of that rationality is located within a Christian context: in St Athanasius' defense of the divinity of the Logos.[29] It is possible that Sharpe has been challenged by the threat posed by Jaki's scholarship to the idea shared by not a few Protestants that science and the Reformation sprang from the same conceptual root. Despite his readiness to "dismiss" Jaki, Sharpe admits Jaki occupies a most important place in current scholarship: "If I am to disagree as much as I do with Jaki's programme for the use of theology in physics I am removing from consideration one of the largest corpora of recent writings in this vein, and give myself the very difficult task of doing something better."[30]

Another Protestant scholar, A. R. Peacocke criticizes Jaki for not distinguishing various types of cyclic notions of time, without enumerating them. Curiously, Peacocke does not see the anti-theological motivations behind the fact that, as he puts it, "most historians of science are hesitant to agree that beliefs in a creator and creation are necessary conditions for the growth of science."[31] At any rate, Jaki carefully distinguished between the need for theology for the birth of science and the very indirect need of it for the growth of an already self-sustaining science. D. C. Allison holds, along with Jaki, that Christianity constituted a matrix for science but regards the absence of science in Eastern Christendom as a proof that the matrix in question was not sufficient.[32] Tellingly, he fails to consider the conceptual limitations which Eastern Christendom imposed on itself through its extreme cultivation of Platonism.

G. S. Hendry also stressed that "the cosmic dimension of theism has been more consistently kept in view in the theology of the Eastern Church than in that of the Western Churches."[33] Again, he too ignores that such a cosmic dimension in Eastern theology was lacking in a metaphysical consideration of the consequences of belief in creation out of nothing and in time. The East did not confront Greek necessitarianism in the same systematic way as was the case with medieval Latin scholasticism. Jaki notes that difference as he writes: "Byzantium largely skirted the issue by withdrawing its orthodoxy into a lofty supernaturalism steeped in Neoplatonism. In such a framework there was no room either for science or for natural theology."[34]

Hendry raises a further problem in writing that "science developed a momentum of its own, and its continued progress stems from the dedication of its practitioners to its intrinsic aims without regard to theological and philosophical implications."[35] Jaki has repeatedly underlined the fact that once science has had a viable birth its future development was assured. However, Jaki also showed — in fact several chapters of his Gifford Lectures are devoted to this point — that whenever the epistemological presuppositions of that birth have been given up or denied, the outcome was potentially threatening to the future of science. As proofs of this Jaki gave a detailed analysis of the implications for science of the scientific method proposed by Bacon, Descartes, Kant, the German idealists, Mach, and, in the the 20th century, by the logical positivists and the paradigmists.[36] Conversely, as Jaki argued in those Lectures, at every truly creative turn in the history of science, an epistemology was in evidence that at least by implication showed affinity with a realist metaphysics. To provide telling examples of this fact, Jaki analyzed in great detail the scientific creativity of Newton, Planck, and Einstein.[37] The latter in particular made statements, mentioned and quoted only by Jaki in the vast literature about Einstein,[38] that forcefully illustrate the theme of this work: extraordinary scientific creativity brings one face to face with the Christian notion of creation.

Another reviewer, F. E. Budenholzer, makes a point that many of the opponents of Jaki's historical thesis would agree with: "Historical analysis does not admit of the simple cause and effect relations of classical physics."[39] Jaki does not reduce physics to its history. This would be historicism which he clearly opposes. Much less does he take history for a set of inevitable steps. However, Jaki would say that the principle of causality operates both in intellectual history (including the history of science) and in the physical world. While in the latter the chain of causality is uninterrupted (he has no use for the fallacies of the Copenhagen interpretation of quantum mechanics), in intellectual history new phases of the chain are introduced by the discoveries of the mind. To deny the operation of causality within those phases would be tantamount to making meaningless the study of history.

T. S. Torrance makes the interesting observation that, in ancient cultures, the inadequacies of the world-view should also have affected areas of life other than science.[40] Jaki has in fact noted how those mistaken world views influenced non-scientific areas and he did so in connection with all ancient cultures. Here let what he stated about the Aztecs suffice: "The background of frightening cosmic cycles with its debilitating fatalism undermined not only the chances of the Aztecs for meaningful cultural advances, but also destroyed their political future."[41] Jaki does not regard science as equally stillborn in all cultures. He notes that ancient Greece came closer to a viable science than any other ancient culture, and its feats in other areas were also extraordinary by comparison. Still, and this is a point to which he returns time and again, much food for thought is provided by the fact that science, this most extraordinary cultural development, is so closely tied to the Christian belief in creation out of nothing and in time. It was that belief that directly sparked the formulation of the idea of inertial motion, the very basis of all science, which is about things in motion.

It is a reflection on the debate under consideration that some reviewers contradict one another other in terms of their own points of view. Thus, for instance, K. F. Thibodeau accuses Jaki of presenting "a lopsided picture of the history of science" and of adopting "a narrow and positivistic point of view."[42] The latter claim should seem preposterous in the light of Jaki's sustained criticism of positivism.[43] If Jaki is so narrow, it is hard to understand W. J. Neidhardt's view that "Dr. Jaki is to be highly commended for his sensitivity, graciousness and fairness in analyzing the religious presuppositions of cultures other than the Judaic-Christian culture of the Western world."[44]

There are indeed many reviewers who agree with Jaki's thesis that science was born from a medieval Christian matrix. Often these commentators do not give their own reasons for their view, but usually restate Jaki's arguments. An exception is P. E. Hodgson who has noted an important progression in Jaki's writings concerning the unique viable birth of science: *The Relevance of Physics* (1966) merely mentions the metaphysical foundations in physics; *Science and Creation* (1974) develops the idea that this metaphysics was essentially absent in all ancient cultures, but present in the medieval Christian matrix; *The Road of Science and the Ways to God* (1978) takes the argument further. There Jaki shows the presence of that metaphysics behind the great creative advances of modern science, such as Newton's system, Planck's quantum theory, and Einstein's relativity. No less importantly, Jaki showed in great detail the potential stifling of scientific creativity whenever that metaphysics is abandoned or denied. Concerning the whole of Jaki's work and his respect for facts, Hodgson concludes: "The central strand in Jaki's work is this respect for all facts, historical and physical, respect for objective knowledge across its full spectrum, of the material world as known by scientists, of the God we know through the material world and through his revelation."[45] Most important among those scientific facts is the legitimate use, through Einstein's cosmology, of the term "universe" in science, a feat which Jaki was the first to discover, so to speak. Of that discovery of his, scientists, as well as historians and philosophers of science, still have to take full consciousness.

The discovery about modern science

While Jaki's reviewers and critics were eager to comment on his views about the medieval origins of modern science, they failed to react to what he considered the most important discovery in the history of science. The discovery consists in two steps. One is Einstein's feat in General Relativity that offers a contradiction-free treatment of the totality of gravitationally interacting matter. This point was the major thrust of Jaki's pioneering study of the entire history of what is usually referred to as Olbers' paradox.[46] In subsequent historical studies, such as the one on the Milky Way[47] and the gravitational paradox,[48] Jaki made repeated references to the crucial bearing of Einstein's achievement for a re-articulation of the cosmological argument. He put this point in particular against the background of Kant's insistence on the invalidity of the notion of the universe as the reason for the invalidity of the cosmological argument.[49] In Jaki's recent work, *God and the Cosmologists*, there is a systematic development of this train of thought[50] whose originality and importance for natural theology cannot be emphasized enough. Recognized by the Templeton-award committee as one of Jaki's crucial contributions, it still has to filter down to the consciousness of scholars — theologians, scientists, and historians and philosophers of science.

Jaki is equally original in exploiting the second step in that discovery. It relates to the specifics established, first through Einstein's General Relativity, and fifty years later through the discovery of the 2.7°K cosmic background radiation, about the entire universe. Just as in connection with the first step, here too Jaki shows the significance of these developments against a historical background. Prior to these developments much credit was given to Laplace's cosmogenesis in which a nebulous, nondescript state of affairs was taken for the primordial starting point. The inherent logical fallacy, that a most specific state of affairs, such as the present state of the universe, could be forthcoming from a homogeneous primordial state, reached its pseudo-philosophical sanctioning in Herbert Spencer's cosmogenesis, a target of Jaki's repeated criticism.[51]. Jaki also shows that such a cosmogenesis could but strengthen the notion that the universe was self-explaining: a homogeneous (nebulous) entity appears to the mind as something that exists naturally and therefore is in no need of further explanation.

Jaki's use of modern scientific cosmology should recommend itself by his care not to look for a "scientific" proof of creation. Although he takes the discovery of the 2.7°K cosmic background radiation for a major evidence on behalf of the expansion of the universe, he does not see in the latter a scientific evidence about a temporal beginning of the universe. A strict temporal beginning of the universe implies for him its creation out of nothing, an event strictly unobservable.[52] For him the vast research which that radiation stimulated about the early history of the universe merely shows that science goes from one specific state of cosmic affairs to another no less specific state as it traces farther and farther back the history of the cosmos. He argues that there is no evidence that science would ever cease to spot a still more primordial state than the one actually under investigation. This is why, among other things, he dismisses talks about the spotting, by science, of the moment of creation. According to him science can establish that the universe is at least so old (say a dozen billions of years), but it cannot measure the absolute age of the universe. The principal philosophical profit which Jaki feels entitled to derive from modern scientific cosmology is the validity of the question posed about the entire cosmos: why such and not something else?

In Jaki's words, "the 2.7°K background radiation ultimately proved not so much that there was an *early* universe . . . but that even in its earliest stages the universe was what a universe had to be: a most specific totality of all things that, because they were things, could only be specific." Even if the way of viewing the early universe changed, it would still be very particular, for "the quantitative specificity of a particular state (or phase or shape) of matter can be traced only to another state no less specific in its quantitative characteristics."[53] The very fact that further discoveries are made in science shows that there is a specificity in the cosmos which is progressively uncovered. Thus the quality of specificity which Jaki sees in the cosmos is non-dependent on a particular scientific finding. Specificity in creation has been seen in the past discoveries of science and will be revealed in its future findings.

Jaki stresses that the specificity of the cosmos is evidence of its reality. Furthermore, "such a specific universe reveals its contingency by its being limited to a specific form of physical existence."[54] If the universe is specific it could have been otherwise, therefore it need not be what it is, therefore it is not necessarily what it happens to be, thus it is contingent. It has been remarked elsewhere that "the idea of specificity in the cosmos can mean that it is determinate, or tuned to a specific purpose or that it is striking in its limitedness."[55] This raises the question of the relation between the physical understanding of specificity and its philosophical interpretation. What is the continuity between the physical and philosophical meanings of specificity? Moreover, are all the meanings of specificity connected with the philosophical notion of contingence? Jaki is most careful in distinguishing the metaphysical level of contingence from its physical expressions when he notes that although physical laws are "expressive of contingent existence . . . they are as such not a grasp of that existence."[56] Jaki stresses that natural objects do not immediately reveal their contingency, and science shows that for such objects "the actual form or structure is the necessary outcome of the interaction of other similarly specific forms."[57] However, for the cosmos as a whole (apart from the question of life) all natural objects are the result of very specific initial conditions. The contingency of the cosmos implies for Jaki that it is but "one of many possible universes."[58] Hence the universe is, in its particular form, dependent on an extra-cosmic choice.

Clearly, Jaki's reflections on the very specific universe, present as well as very early, are very different from what one finds in works written for wider consumption by scientific cosmologists, whose views he had systematically criticized in his 1989 Oxford Lectures, *God and the Cosmologists*. He has no use for the anti-metaphysical inferences which A. H. Guth drew from his inflationary theory in spite of its usefulness to explain, say, the horizon problem. No physical theory, Jaki warned already in connection with the steady-state theory, entitles the physicist to postulate creation out of nothing as part of actual physical processes. Much less is he willing to see anything rational in Guth's claim that the inflationary theory enables the physicist to create universes "literally out of nothing."[59]

Nor does Jaki condone the inclination of not a few cosmologists to doubt the connection of their work about the early universe with its physical reality. One such cosmologist is S. Weinberg who wrote: "I cannot deny a feeling of unreality in writing about the first three minutes as if we really know what we are talking about." Clearly, this does not accord with his statement that the testing of theoretical ideas in physics and astrophysics has become a "common language which allows theorists and observers to appreciate what each other are doing."[60] The fact of a development in models about the cosmos in no way undermines Jaki's reflections which are independent of particulars in that development. He is most conscious of the limited validity of each stage in the progress of science and would be wary of regarding any phase of science as definitively final, let alone necessarily so.

Jaki certainly does not take for a final step a possible eventual advance beyond the barrier posed by Planck's time or 10^{-43} seconds. As is well known, General Relativity implies a singularity, that is, some form of infinite force or energy, when extended beyond that time. Jaki would, however, note the contradictory character of such comments as the one offered by Barrow and Tipler: "Prior to the Planck time 10^{-43}s we know nothing of the state of space and time nor even if such familiar entities existed; neither quantum theory nor general relativity are valid before this time, the entire Universe is a quantum phenomenon, and a major extension of physics — the theory of quantum gravity — will be necessary before anything sensible can be said of these moments."[61] Clearly, if quantum theory is not valid beyond that phase, it is not justified to speak, in the same breath, of the universe as a quantum phenomenon. Apart from this, as he argued in *God and the Cosmologists*, any treatment of the universe as a quantum phenomenon implies the multiplication of universes, too high a price to pay for the destruction of the notion of the universe itself as a strict totality.[62]

It is clear that the formulation of the various models of the cosmos presupposes a relationship between the observational and theoretical realms of physics. The discovery of the 2.7°K cosmic background radiation is within the realm of experimental physics: an extrapolation to the earlier history of the cosmos requires a combination of empirical evidence and hypothesis. The basis of the argument lies in the interrelation between various branches of physical science: astronomy, relativity, quantum mechanics, nuclear reactions and thermodynamics. There is therefore always a relation with the observable in all respectable models of cosmic history. However there are limits of verification within cosmology. The limitations within scientific cosmology would be clearly admitted by Jaki as has been seen in Chapter Two.

Jaki is careful to avoid the facile interpretation which would necessarily invoke an act of creation as a ground for the state of the universe which is the earliest stage under actual investigation, the one immediately prior to Planck's time. Such an interpretation is lurking behind Weinberg's remark that "although we do not know that it is true, it is at least logically possible that there *was* a beginning, and that time itself has no meaning before that moment."[63] Jaki would insist that it is outside the competence of science to arrive at the very first moment in time, for to do so it would have to investigate the boundary between time and that which lies outside time (at the point where time = 0). Science is incapable of dealing with the time/non-time boundary: this is part of the radical limitation of science in relation to philosophy. In Jaki's words: "The method of physics always means an inference from one observable state to another."[64]

Science is always advancing; that which is unknown today is discovered tomorrow. Thus Jaki is entirely consistent in not ascribing the work of creation to the initial singularity. What Jaki actually does in interpreting the 2.7°K radiation is to see its consequences within science and philosophy before applying the results to theology. The process involves the construction of a broad and secure scientific base before making any metaphysical deductions. It would be an unwarranted extension of science to use scientific data directly in a philosophical or theological argument. Hodgson clearly reflects Jaki's arguments as he remarks that the relationship between "scientific and theological beliefs is not a simple one, certainly not one that allows a compelling deduction from one to the other."[65]

The quality of specificity lies at the level of the relationship between matter and form, while the quality of contingency concerns the level of the connection between essence and existence. The road of contingency is therefore one which cannot be traversed by science alone: the use of philosophy is required. In particular, the key step in this road is the Thomistic principle that the existence of beings grounds knowledge.[66] Then"every step of real knowledge is a step to something different" and "the proof of such steps is that knowledge which is to know things and to know them to be known."[67] In this realist perspective, there is a clear difference between numbers and things and also between logic and things. As Jaki argues,[68] Hawking fails to distinguish precisely between a physical notion of singularity and its metaphysical consequences vis-à-vis God the Creator. At one time he held that there was an initial singularity, but more recently he has changed his mind. Hawking appears to interpret the Uncertainty Principle in a way which gives it an ontological status instead of a purely operational status, a difference which Jaki has repeatedly pointed out.[69] Only by ignoring this difference does it become possible to have matter appear and disappear without a Creator in the manner of the logical theft already noted in Chapter Three.

Hawking assumes that the universe is finite but unbounded. He states that his idea that space and time are finite but without a boundary is "just a *proposal*: it cannot be deduced from some other principle." The proposal is supposed to square well with the quantum theory of gravity, where it is difficult to see whether theory agrees with observations. Nevertheless on the strength of this proposal, Hawking remarks that "there would be no singularities at which the laws of science broke down and no edge of space-time at which one would have to appeal to God."[70] Hawking wishes to deny the existence of God by a "God of the gaps" argument, for it is clear that God is removed by dispensing with the points where physics breaks down. This is a deistic vision of God, one where his providential presence within the cosmos is denied. This is also a vision which makes science complete in itself, not requiring any explanation outside itself. Jaki notes that Hawking does not refer to Gödel's theorems; this is all the more significant since, as Jaki argues, "the chief bearing of Gödel's theorems on cosmology" is "that the contingency of the cosmos cannot be contradicted."[71] On the basis of his flimsy presuppositions Hawking states that the universe "would just BE," not as a contingent but as a necessary entity. In this way he seems to banish the Creator from the cosmos with the boastful question: "What place, then, for a creator?"[72]

Quite differently, Jaki uses the specificity of the universe for a metaphysical inference to its contingency, an inference not based on facile use of science. In fact, he points out time and again that what has been learned through modern scientific cosmology merely strengthens the evidence available to common sense as the latter reveals the specificity of everything. Of course, he keeps noting that in view of the premium set in modern culture on scientific information, the precision which science reveals about the specificity of each and every thing, and of their totality, should seem a most persuasive contribution. Science depends on common sense taken in its best metaphysical meaning already when it assumes the existence of things so that it may establish their quantitative specificities. Even greater is that dependence of science, to continue with a fundamental aspect of Jaki's argumentation, when it assumes the reality of the universe so that it may offer a scientific cosmology about it.[73]

In sum, Jaki makes careful distinctions between what is science, what is logic, and what is metaphysics. Through a realist metaphysics, he argues, it is possible to make the step from the specificity of the cosmos to its contingency and thence to the existence of God. In effect, Jaki uses metaphysics as a kind of bridge between science and theology. This indicates a solidity of approach, for it means that science and theology are left intact, respecting the nature proper to each. Jaki's method is one which seeks more than a transient appeal as he relates science to the Christian theology of creation via a realist philosophy. It is this realist philosophy and the christological thrust of Jaki's theology of creation which will be examined in the next chapter.

7

The Crucial Thrust

There is but one thought greater than that of the universe, and
that is the thought of its Maker.

John Henry Newman, *The Idea of a University*

The appraisal of Jaki's approach to Christian belief in God the
Creator in relation to science has centered on two trains of thought.
The philosophical one dealt with the contribution which modern
science made, with its concrete grasp of the cosmos, to the theological
appreciation of faith in God the Creator. The other train of thought
concerned the impact of Christian faith in God the Creator on the
unique historical birth of science. These two related lines of enquiry
will now be pursued further because they cast a sharp light on the
crucial thrust of Jaki's thought. This chapter has therefore to deal first
with the philosophical realism espoused by Jaki and then with his
interpretation of the christological part of theology as a means to
account for the unique viable birth of science.

The realist perspective

Philosophical realism is the metaphysical bridge linking science with
Christian belief in God the Creator, a belief crucial, both historically
and analytically, for Jaki's interpretation of science. He reveals much

of his realism through his criticism of such philosophical interpretations of science as nominalism, positivism, instrumentalism and idealism. Nominalism, which is best portrayed against the medieval controversy about universals, is taken up by Jaki in his discussion of the viable birth of science through the work of Buridan and Oresme. That controversy was a reaction to Plato's view in which the universals were so many instances of an absolute realism: the universal concept is being itself and the role of the mind is solely to discern this being.

In the Platonism of the School of Chartres considerable credence was given to this exaggerated realism or ultra-realism. In this perspective "our generic and specific concepts correspond to a reality existing extramentally in objects, a subsistent reality in which individuals share."[1] In his debate with the ultra-realist, William of Champeaux, Peter Abelard distinguished between the logical and real orders though without denying the objective foundation of the universal concept. Abelard was therefore part of the movement which ultimately lead to Thomistic moderate realism. The latter is thematically endorsed in the principal thesis of Jaki's Gifford Lectures. There he claims on the one hand that the epistemological "stepping stones to God" as embodied in Thomas' five proofs of the existence of God, served as "the stepping stones to science."[2] In other words, he claims that the epistemology underlying those proofs is the same one that was needed for the viable birth of science and remains present in its creative advances. Conversely, he defends the same epistemology by portraying in detail the potentially disastrous consequences in store for science whenever a different epistemology is taken for its methodology. This is not to suggest that Jaki enters into the specifics of Thomas' view that "universals are virtually present in individuals, from which they are abstracted by our intellect," or into the nuances of Scotus' claim that the universals are "real entities apart from their existence in individuals."[3]

Early in the century of Buridan and Oresme a markedly anti-realist solution to the question of universals was given by William of Ockham. For Ockham and the nominalists there are no universal realities outside the mind. Man only encounters individually existing entities without being able to arrive at a unity of meaning for entities that form, in all appearance, one class. The nominalists reduced each universal to a word (whether mental, spoken or written) which is itself an individual entity. Jaki rejects any strong link between the medieval scientific tradition originated by Buridan and Oresme (whatever their nominalist phraseologies) and Ockham. He does so for two reasons. One is that both Buridan and Oresme endorsed the cosmological argument which rests on the reality of that foremost of unobservable universals which is the universe, an argument unacceptable to Ockham as pointedly noted by Jaki.[4] He further notes in this connection that Ockham was forced by his nominalism into a rejection of univeral laws operative in nature and expressive of a causal interaction among the universality of things.[5] Such criticism is meaningful only from the perspective of a realist standpoint. Equally revealing of that standpoint is Jaki's contestation of the view that interest in empirical observation began with Ockham's nominalism and not through the moderate realist Scholastic tradition: "Well before Ockham the investigation of particulars was emphasized by Albertus Magnus, Roger Bacon, Witelo, Theodoric of Freiberg, and others."[6]

Jaki's preference for moderate realism is the guiding principle as he traces the instinctive epistemological middle road which was adopted by Newton in doing science.[7] The latter point is not without originality in that Jaki also shows the rationalist (Cartesian) and empiricist (Baconian) heritage which Newton retained in his non-scientific hours.[8] Again, much is revealed about Jaki's realism through his systematic portrayal of the scientific nullity of Auguste Comte's positive philosophy. Comte hoped that his positivism would, in conjunction with the positive sciences, give the complete answer to all the questions that can be rightfully raised about man and the cosmos. But since for Comte knowledge is limited to sense experience, he had to deny scientific status to observations mediated by microscope and telescopes. Any such mediated knowledge had, for Comte, the touch of metaphysics to it, a *bête noire* in his positivist outlook. He was, as Jaki showed convincingly, willing to pay, in support of his positivism, even the price of deriding stellar astronomy, to say nothing of cosmology.[9]

It is the same concern for universally valid scientific laws, arguable only on the basis of a realist metaphysics, that forms the central point of Jaki's criticism of the phenomenological positivism of J. S. Mill. To show the basic inadequacy of Mill's theory of knowledge as the complex of actual and possible sensations, Jaki recalls an apparently incidental but highly revealing claim of Mill about the possibility of other worlds in which two and two do not necessarily make four.[10] Similar is the method of Jaki's endorsement of realism as he takes on 20th-century forms of positivism, such as logical positivism and operationism. The claim of logical positivists that only those statements are valid which can be translated into propositions of physics, he counters with examples that show that claim's self-defeating character.[11] As to the failure of operationism to cope with reality in its full range, Jaki illustrates this by calling attention to P. W. Bridgman's claim that cosmology is nonsensical and that astronomy should limit its range of observation to a few thousand light years.[12]

Needless to say, as a historian and philosopher of science Jaki has a direct interest in some major trends of the philosophy of science in this century. A chief reason for this lies with his vast studies on Pierre Duhem who is often represented in those trends as a positivist understudy of Ernst Mach. Jaki's criticism of Mach's sensationism centers on its non-realist and antimetaphysical aspects, and in particular on Mach's scorn for cosmology.[13] As to Duhem's positivism, Jaki relentlessly argued that, in the very words of Duhem, it was a mere method based on the explicit acceptance of some realist, and in fact most metaphysical presuppositions.[14] Particularly noteworthy in this respect is Jaki's study of Duhem's early philosophical writings, full of thematic endorsements of a realist epistomology and metaphysics.[15] The sympathy with which Jaki recalls those statements reflects Jaki's realism as well.

Were not Jaki a realist he would not have invariably distanced himself from the non-realist epistemological interpretations of the history of science propounded by T. S. Kuhn and others.[16] If Kuhn is a major target of Jaki's it is not so much because Kuhn's casting the history of science into a succession of incommensurable paradigms destroys the idea of scientific progress. It is rather because Jaki sees beneath progress, scientific or other, a far greater intellectual commodity: a continuity in material and thought processes that alone assures meaning to change, this most fundamental of all philosophical challenges that lies at the origin of all debates about the universals.[17] A further indication of Jaki's genuinely metaphysical realism is his criticism of Holton's advocacy of a "rationalist" metaphysics[18] and of the claims that reliance on specious words, such as "themata," "images" and "research programs," answers basic epistemological questions.[19] Jaki's metaphysical realism comes through in his critique of Wittgenstein's efforts to turn concepts into images of things.[20] Much of Jaki's "Language, Logic, Logos" is an articulation of themes of realist metaphysics which, according to him, is the sole means of countering the mirage of artificial intelligence.[21] According to him the idea of such an intelligence is not a scientific matter but a purely philosophical one, and a most mistaken one, to boot.[22]

Jaki's realism is the reason for his sustained and repeated criticism of the idealist interpretations of modern science, especially as championed by A. S. Eddington.[23] According to Jaki a chief danger of idealism is its lure toward an a priori account of nature, a lure that encroaches on Einstein's groping towards a genuine realism, which Jaki portrayed with great sympathy.[24]

It took the thorough realist in Jaki to oppose, almost single-handedly for more than a decade now, the Copenhagen interpretation of quantum mechanics with a specifically articulated argument on behalf of realism. In doing so Jaki went far beyond such critics of that interpretation as Einstein, who merely deplored, as Jaki noted (though with thorough approval), the "risky game" which the Copenhagen people were playing with reality.[25] Unlike Einstein and others, Jaki did not try to overcome that interpretation by arguing the possibility of a fully "deterministic" physics. As a genuine ontological realist he clearly saw that the Copenhagen denial of ontological causality rests on a fallacy in reasoning which he summed up as the following *non-sequitur*: an interaction that cannot be measured "exactly" cannot take place "exactly." The fallacy is the inference from a purely operational meaning of "exactly" to a distinctly ontological one.

As a truly ontological realist Jaki clearly saw that insofar as a "deterministic" physics means the possibility of perfectly accurate measurements, it merely assumes that there is an ontologically accurate causal interaction between physical things. Jaki kept arguing that ontological accuracy is the very ground of accurate interactions, regardless of whether physicists will ever have the tools, conceptual or real, of measuring those interactions accurately.[26] A further aspect of this is Jaki's warning against taking the indeterminacy principle either for an assurance about the free will of man[27] or for the possibility of miracles.[28]

Jaki's realism sustains his criticism of Bohr's philosophy of complementarity. He compares it graphically to the sketching of two sides of a face that need not rest in a real head.[29] It is Jaki who kept recalling the conclusion of a major study of Bohr's philosophy, namely, that its gist is the systematic avoidance of questions of ontology.[30] Jaki, who noticed in full the pragmatism lurking beneath the surface of Bohr's writings, could more easily confront it in the writings of William James and of process philosophers, especially of Bergson, Alexander, and Whitehead.[31] The same is true of his strictures of those who sought in "emergence" an explanation of radically new aspects of reality.[32] All those strictures have at their source his respect for reality as a matter far too serious to be left to arcane play with words.

As may be expected, Jaki found no philosophical depth in Teilhard de Chardin's writings that offer the "Catholic" variety of the philosophy of emergence.[33] He found in those writings a deluge of metaphors aimed at skirting questions of ontology. Nor did he show sympathy for transcendental Thomism for which he coined the word, "Aqui-Kantism," as a reminder of its hybrid character and heavy indebtedness to Kant's subjectivist antirealism.[34] As to the danger which transcendental Thomism poses for Catholic thought, Jaki spoke of it all too clearly in his introduction to the English translation of Etienne Gilson's small epistemological masterpiece on methodical realism.[35] In a recent book of his, *The Purpose of It All*, Jaki relied in fact on that touchstone of Thomist realism which is the doctrine of analogy in order to show the manner in which "purpose" can be attributed to the activity of purely biological entities.[36]

In view of all this one should easily see the extent to which a reviewer of Jaki's Gifford Lectures missed the target in saying that Jaki's own philosophical position, "which seems to be based on the neo-scholasticism of writers such as Jacques Maritain and Etienne Gilson, is never really spelled out. Process philosophers (e.g. Alfred North Whitehead) and the transcendental Thomists (e.g. Bernard Lonergan) would interpret the history of science in a similar vein and also hold a realist view of epistemology and metaphysics. Yet the details and conclusions of their analysis would be quite different from Jaki's. The position of moderate realism is not quite so 'self- evident' as the author seems to believe."[37]

Jaki is not alone with his claim that process philosophers and transcendental Thomists are not realists. As to the claim that Loner-gan, for instance, would offer an interpretation of the history of

science similar to his, Jaki could easily dismiss it with the simple
remark that Lonergan nowhere offered such an interpretation. As to
Lonergan's excursions into the philosophy of science, Jaki spoke of
them as being either factually wrong or simply amateurish.[38] For the
purposes he had set himself, Jaki did not have to go into minuter
details of realist epistemology. His purpose was to uncover the major
features of the intellectual landscape which is the philosophical
interpretation of the history of science. He found that landscape
buried under layers of clichés forged since the early 17th century, and
especially since the coming of the Encyclopedists, and even more so
during our own century. He would gladly leave to others the
working out the small particulars about the true contours of that
landscape.

In tracing that landscape Jaki is guided by John Henry Newman's remark about theological history, a remark which he is fond of
quoting: "History is not a creed or catechism, it gives lessons rather
than rules; still no one can mistake its general teaching. . . . Bold
outlines and broad masses of colour rise out of the records of the past.
They may be dim, they may be incomplete but they are definite."
Jaki would consider fully applicable to his claims the continuation of
Newman's remark: "And this one thing at least is certain; whatever
history teaches, whatever it omits, whatever it exaggerates or
extenuates, whatever it says and unsays, at least the Christianity of
history is not Protestantism. If ever there were a safe truth, it is
this."[39] According to Jaki whatever history teaches about science, or
rather about the philosophy in terms of which science achieved its
birth and great advances, that philosophy was not a sort of idealism,
operationism, and pragmatism but genuine realism, merely implicit as
it could be in the thinking of great scientists. He would claim: "If
ever there were a safe truth, it is this." For a proof he would refer to
such giants of the historical landscape of science as Newton, Planck
and Einstein.

He found it most revealing that the last two, one "at most a
nominal Christian," the other "an agnostic Jew,"[40] were at least
recognizing, precisely because of their leanings towards realism, the
possible bearing of their findings for theism.[41] At any rate, as Jaki
argued, explicit theism need not be part of the scientific enterprise
once it has arisen from a realist as well as explicitly Christian
epistemological matrix. This is why non-Christians can be metaphys-

ical realists in their science at least. They witness thereby to man's
natural tendency toward realism as an assurance of intellectual insight,
although it is a tendency which, Jaki noted, has been weakened by
original sin.[42]

Needless to say, in speaking about common sense perception as
the very basis of epistemologial realism, Jaki had no intention to
improve on Gilson's masterly analysis of the correct and false
meanings of that term.[43] But he is quite original concerning the
most inclusive object of that realism, the universe. His definition of
the universe as "the totality of consistently interacting things"[44] can
serve science as well as philosophy. It is certainly a major improve-
ment over scholastic cosmologies that, as he pointed out, all too often
contain no chapter on the cosmos as such.[45] His defense of the
universe as the most precious object of human reason against agnostic
and flippant remarks[46] is a logical part of his principal interest in the
universe. It is for him the springboard from which metaphysical
realism enables man to rise to the recognition of the contingency of
the cosmos and beyond it, of the existence of God the Creator.
Assertion of the non-necessary character of the cosmos is a distinctive
feature in the Christian notion of creation. However, it is its
christological dimension that especially sets the Christian vision of
creation apart from all other world views, a point now to be discussed in some detail.

Christology and cosmos

If one takes seriously, as Jaki does, the expression "Christian view of
the cosmos," one is obliged to take a momentous though nuanced
position. The respect enjoined by Vatican II for all religions and
cultures makes it already a sensitive matter to talk, even with no
reference to Christology, about the strictly created character of the
universe to representatives of Confucianism, Buddhism and Hinduism
— all pantheists in one way or another. The problem is aggravated by
the pride which members of such religions take in their being heirs
to great ancient cultures. The dialogue with them can include, if at
all, only at a much later stage a reference to Christ in the fulness of
His mystery, or the creation of all in Him and through Him.

However, the Catholic theologian who engages in that dialogue
in this age of science may find a good starting point in calling
attention to a general feature of all those cultures insofar as they are

embodied in a modern political state. In all such states a feverish effort has been going on for the past century or so to catch up scientifically and technologically with the Western world. If then the Catholic theologian is allowed to raise the question why those non-Western cultures had failed in science, he may recall points set forth by Jaki in great detail about the relation of pantheism to science. In Jaki's works the theologian can find, for instance, clearly articulated the conceptual difficulty of formulating, within a pantheistic context, the first law of motion, this most fundamental among of all scientific laws about a world in which everything is in motion.[47]

In the dialogue with representatives of non-Christian monotheism, such as Judaism and Islam, the christological dimension comes in at a very early stage, if not immediately. Here the Catholic theologian in charge of the dialogue could be considerably aided if he were to use Jaki's portrayal of a feature common to intellectuals in both of those religions. From the moment when Jewish and Muslim intellectuals became acquainted with Aristotelian pantheism, many of them found it well-nigh impossible to resist its lure.[48] If then one is allowed to broach the question why medieval Jews and Muslims failed to formulate that all-important first law of motion and thereby make the breakthrough toward a viable science, it becomes possible to demand a favorable hearing for Christology.

Christians and Catholics still have to realize in depth the significance, repeatedly insisted upon by Jaki, of the expression "only begotten Son,"[49] which, as predicated about a concrete human being, serves as a powerful barrier against taking the world for another "begetting" or emanation from the divine. Since such an emanation has to be, logically speaking, a necessary process, and has been such in all emanationist systems, from Plotinus to Hegel, Christology implies the absolute freedom of God to create.

It is indeed most significant that in the decades preceding the work of Buridan and Oresme, much attention was paid to the condemnation in 1277 by Etienne Tempier, bishop of Paris, of a number of Aristotelian theses. Having been issued in Paris, then the center of Christian intellectualism, the condemnation certainly strengthened awareness of the sovereignty of the divine will. The rise, during the 15th century, of Italian Averroism, may have prompted the emphatic reassertion, by the Council of Florence, of God's freedom to create: God is "the Creator of all things, visible and invisible, who, when He so willed, out of His bounty made all creatures, spiritual as well as corporeal."[50] The resurgence of pantheism through Hegelian idealism played a part in the reassertion, at Vatican I, of the same freedom of God.[51]

Among the consequences of this affirmation is that God is free not to have created anything. Still another consequence is that God could have created the cosmos otherwise and that therefore the world could have taken on any number of possible forms. Thus the present particular form must be highly specific, differing from other possible forms of the cosmos, and hence cannot be fathomed *a priori* by mental introspection, but only by an *a posteriori* empirical investigation. The Christian concept of God's freedom to create was therefore, as Jaki argued, a stimulus for scientific investigation of contingent scientific laws, namely "only one among an infinitely large number of possible sets of laws."[52] Clearly, Jaki argues something much more than the point, often made before him, that monotheism, or its doctrine of creation, implies a world that has to be investigated in a *non a priori* manner. What Jaki argues specifically is that Christian monotheism was able to put these points across, and still make them meaningful, precisely because that monotheism is Christ-centered.

A further aspect of Jaki's argument is the link between the notion of the freedom of God and His creating in time. To quote Jaki: "Creation in time is an evidence of God's absolute freedom to create."[53] This quote alone should indicate that Jaki's presentation of creation in time has nothing in common with its misunderstanding by some modern scientific cosmologists, such as Hawking. According to the latter, if a cosmological model includes an initial singularity, "God would still have had complete freedom to choose what had happened and how the universe began." Apart from the deistic flavor of Hawking's "concession" to God, it also contains the deistic logic, that had fully run its course, as Jaki showed, within 19th-century materialism. The deists had denied to God true freedom to create long before Hawking declared that "God had no freedom at all to choose initial conditions."[54] To "evict God" is Jaki's concise summary of Hawking's real aim.[55] The universe of deists and of Hawking has to be what it is, or rather appears to be necessary, given some aprioristic assumptions either about matter or about the laws of mathematical physics.

Another contribution of orthodox, dogmatic Christology is, according to Jaki, a strong appreciation of time as actually experienced. That the Incarnation took place at a fixed point of time, marked by the invariable reference to Pontius Pilate in all credal formulas, could but enhance the perception of the uniqueness of each moment and therefore of history. Since such uniqueness is inconceivable within the recurrence of cyclic ages, the Incarnation added further emphasis to a linear perception of time, which had been an integral part of Old Testament salvation history. Still, the difference between an event, such as the calling of Abraham or of Moses, and the taking of flesh by the Son of God, should seem enormous from the viewpoint of uniqueness. Jaki notes that a modern continuous calendar, which was inconceivable within some ancient cultures,[56] became imperative within the Judeo–Christian framework.

Yet, here too, the impact of Christianity was liberating. Were it not for Christianity, the Western world would still operate with two calendars, both very much in vogue until the first decades of the 18th century. One of them, the Jewish counting of the years of history in terms of a literal reading of Old Testament chronology, would be most embarrassing today when the age of the universe is measured in billions of years and the age of mankind in a few million years. The other, or the counting of years since the foundation of Rome, could not have posed an effective barrier to efforts, inspired by various types of chauvinism, aimed at setting a new starting point, such as the storming of the Bastille or of the Winter Palace. Against this background something more than a natural factor, as Jaki notes,[57] may transpire from the fact that the counting of the years of history with reference to the birth of Christ, became an exclusive custom in Europe only a few decades prior to the French Revolution.

In his reflections on God's freedom to create, Jaki is clearly in that medieval scholastic tradition which reached its ultimate refinement, to recall the words of M. Schmaus, in Scotus's stress "on the absolute freedom of the divine plan for creation. No other medieval theologian succeeded in emphasizing the freedom of God to the extent that he did without lapsing into the notion of an arbitrary God."[58] What prevented theologians like St. Thomas and Scotus from drifting into voluntarism is that the divine freedom and divine rationality were seen by them in relation to one another. Their balanced view was opposed by Ockham's occasionalist voluntarism whose disastrous methodology of science is the repeated target of Jaki's criticism.

As to the rationality of the cosmos, its erstwhile perception is traced by Jaki, in one of his most original findings, to Athanasius' anti-Arian reflections on the dogma of the Incarnation. Only with faith in that dogma, to quote Jaki, there came "a categorical assertion about the full rationality of a world created by a fully divine Logos."[59] This claim may seem to conflict with Catholic tradition grounded in Scripture, that man can arrive at the notion of a true Creator, whose work has to be fully rational, through the power of unaided reason.[60] Yet this perception of a fully rational cosmos cannot be found among the Greeks, the creators of the most rational culture among all ancient cultures. Does this mean that the possibility in question is more theoretical than practical?

Jaki sought an answer to this question with a detailed reference in *The Savior of Science* to original sin, a reference particularly courageous at a time when that sin is far from being a favorite topic for theologians. The latter are in fact often ready to follow secular thinking which is most reluctant to ascribe lack of good intention to proponents of plain errors. Jaki upholds views more in line with theological tradition than with new thinking as he claims that the Fall inflicted a greater wound on man's will than on man's intellect. He therefore leaves open the possibility that, for instance, the Greeks of old failed to follow up their momentary sightings of creation out of nothing for a reason that had to do less with their mind than with their will. He, of course, does not give comfort to those still echoing the Reformers and the Jansenists. They keep exaggerating the effects of the Fall so that the grace given in Christ may be extolled all the more and even in respect to matters that are purely rational in themselves, such as science. Only a few of them dare to admit at least to themselves that such a stance has, since Luther and Calvin, been the harbinger of plain naturalism.[61]

The opposite position in which Christ is turned into a goal-product of a perennialy evolving Nature, writ large, is certainly not to Jaki's liking. While he always distinguished between Teilhard de Chardin's personal orthodoxy and his speculations about a cosmic Christ,[62] he expressed his anxiety about the logical implications of not a few of Teilhard's statements and of his metaphors.[63] Jaki would hardly go along with statements, more rhetorical than cogently argued, in which, with an eye on Origen and Teilhard de Chardin, Christ is described as "the one who . . . exercises over the universe a supremacy which is physical and not simply juridical [because] He is the unifying center of the cosmos and its goal."[64] Jaki would merely point out that God's creative act is metaphysical and not physical and he would also call attention to the misunderstandings caused by the use of the word "physical" in describing the efficacy of grace.

Given the importance of the part played by Revelation and grace in the actual rise of science, can one exclude the possibility, outside the Christian cultural matrix, for a rise of science which would have been slower and less imposing than is the actual case? Is not such a question justified by the reassertion at Vatican II that grace is given also outside the visible confines of the Church?[65] A possible answer to this question, not raised by Jaki, may be found in his views about the medieval birth of science. The latter he sees as the fruit of an almost thousand-year-long preparation that began when the Church became, after Constantine, a part of the general culture and had to take a direct interest in the empirical and historical aspects of reality and was chiefly responsible for them for many centuries. But that interest had to take on, through the establishment of medieval monastic schools and universities, an institutional strength in order to make possible a proper reaction to Aristotelian pantheism.[66] This institutional preparation failed to take place, even in purely natural terms, in ancient cultures, including Greece.

Jaki's insistence on the spiritual and intellectual superiority of Christian culture is not in conflict with the teaching of Vatican II about the respect due to other cultures steeped in other religions. For the teaching in question restricts that respect "to what is true and holy in these religions." Such is the condition for the high regard demanded from the Church in the same context "for the manner of life and conduct, the precepts and doctrines which, although differing in many ways from her own teaching, nevertheless often reflect a ray of that truth which enlightens all men."[67] Moreover, the same Council also states that Christian Revelation "purges of evil associations those elements of truth and grace which are found among peoples." Therefore a process of conversion is required not only in individuals, but also by the particular culture as a whole. The Council also recalls that this cultural conversion to Christianity has in the past had material as well as spiritual effects for, "even in the secular history of mankind the Gospel has acted as a leaven in the interests of liberty and progress."[68]

Jaki's vision, which at first sight may not appear "ecumenical," is therefore very much in line with the teaching of the Council. He has always noted a limited progress in ancient cultures. Conversely, he also warned that modern progress can be saved from its runaway logic only by recovering a transcendent sense of purpose.[69] He is certainly not a Western chauvinist in the imperialist and colonizing tradition. Nor is he ashamed of the cultural role of the Catholic Church. He showed that the effect of Christian faith in God the Creator on human civilization has been of colossal proportions. He has challenged the opponents of Christianity, who claim that the world is no better since the advent of the Christian gospel, by taking them on in their stronghold, their wilful expropriation of science. He also challenged the claim, very fashionable nowadays, that the scientific progress stimulated by Christianity has brought about a possible ecological disaster.[70] It was with an eye to that charge, whose spokesmen are very reluctant to give credit to Christianity for the birth of science, that Jaki spoke of the "uses and abuses of technology,"[71] and of the difference between ecology and ecologism.[72] He also described modern secularized society as heading toward anarchy as a result of its having replaced ethical principles with mere patterns of behavior.[73] He was not afraid to expose the intellectual shame of the argument according to which AIDS is but a natural epidemic that has to be accepted for mere behavioral and biological reasons.[74] It was with a similar courage that ten years earlier, in his Gifford Lectures, he charged modern society with hypocrisy in standing up for the seventh commandment, while flouting all the others.[75]

Jaki not only showed the colossal contribution of Christian faith to modern scientific society but also the enormous need of that society of the same faith as expressive of a moral philosophy as well. In line with Chesterton's dictum that the dogma about original sin is the most empirical of all Christian dogmas,[76] he offered no utopian perspectives about a scientific future. Yet he has not been preaching either to those outside the Church or to those inside it. He has always argued his case by marshalling a vast array of facts of scientific and intellectual history in order to promote the return of modern scientific culture to its Christian origins. He did this in two phases which, however, he did not plan in advance. In his earlier writings, beginning with *The Relevance of Physics*, he addressed himself mainly to the largely secularist scientific community. He reminded that community about the ability of the Babe born in Bethlehem to create a greater stir than science did.[77] He restricted himself mostly to the theme that physics has but a very limited relevance in the broader context of culture and that in several principal areas of reflection physics, or exact science, has no relevance at all, or only an extremely limited one. He also illustrated this limitedness of physics with his great monographs on the history of astronomy and cosmology.

The Gifford Lectures stand at a turning point of his reflections. There he still pays much attention to the failures of various types of scientific method, a theme that should be of direct interest to a scientist, however indifferent, though not hostile, to historical Christianity. Such a scientist may at least perceive through wading through that book the subtly profound and decisive support which science gained not so much from the so-called "worldly philosophers" but from Christian reflections. Jaki's book, *Cosmos and Creator*, published in 1980 shows him turning towards a theme, anticipated in his *Science and Creation* published in 1974. Both works are much more helpful in strengthening and enlightening Christian, and especially Catholic, intellectuals than in shaking the convictions of their secularist counterparts. With the publication of his great monograph on Pierre Duhem, he served evidence of Samuel Butler's remark that all books are in a sense autobiographical.[78] Jaki shows profound sympathy for Duhem, the great Catholic intellect, who had been slighted or given the silent treatment by the academic establishment and, time and again, even by Catholic intellectuals all too eager to be accepted by prominent members of it. Readers of his most recent book on Duhem, the man of science and of the Catholic faith,[79] will find much eye-opening material there about that situation which is nothing short of being scandalous.[80]

It is therefore understandable that several of the ten or so books Jaki published during the last half a dozen years have in view an audience which he does not have to convince first about the perennial value — intellectual, moral, and cultural — of Christian heritage. To them he speaks with great openness about specific Christian dogmas in their relation to science. He obviously enjoys the task of arguing within the ecclesial ambience and of making those within it aware of their immense possibilities, so far largely left unexploited and assimilated. The agreement of his discourse with the words of the official spokesmen of that ambience will form the topic of the last and concluding chapter.

8

The Ecclesial Perspective

For nearly two thousand years the Church has professed and
constantly proclaimed the truth that the creation of the visible and
invisible world is the work of God. . . . The Church explains and
deepens this truth, using the philosophy of being and defends it
from the errors which arise now and again in human thought.
Pope John Paul II, Address at General Audience,
January 29, 1986.

This work has sought to examine Jaki's views on creation and
scientific creativity. Philosophically, they rest on the proposition that
science is possible because the entities studied by it are believed to
form an orderly whole, a cosmos, accessible to human reason. Jaki
endeavored to show, partly through his analysis of the history of
scientific cosmology, that the specific laws which govern the cosmos
do not form a self-explanatory system. They rather point beyond
science and call for a metaphysical foundation in the Christian
doctrine of creation. It is precisely this doctrine which, according to
Jaki, was the stimulus for the unique viable birth of science. The
Christian notion of creation has for its matrix the Church, the
mystical body of Christ, the "sign and instrument . . . of communion
with God and of unity among all men."[1] It is in the context of the
Church that theologians seek to understand the various propositions

of the Creed. The answer to the question about the manner in which Jaki's work is relevant and faithful to the teaching mission of the Church will place his thought within that ecclesial dimension.

The pastoral mission of the Church

The views on the relevance of Jaki's work to Christian thought in this age of science should be expected to vary greatly. To begin with, philosophical and cultural interpretations of science are of a great variety. More importantly, in this age of ecumenism, it has become a "scholarly" custom to fall back on an artful glossing over of specifics. Cultivators of this custom could but feel rankled by Jaki's relentless insistance on specifics. Worse, his bent on specifics did not relate to matters theological alone. Much of his work related to precisely those specifics that matter most in this age of science when almost everything has to be given a scientific wrapping. Insofar as theological liberalism has retained any ties with Christian tradition, it has now for almost two centuries been much more concerned about appearing "scientific" than about giving the specifics about its Christian character.

The credal points, or rather their vagueness, that underlie Sharpe's slighting of the import of Jaki's work for Christian thought can, however, be guessed with fair accuracy. If a Christian theologian cannot talk with sympathy of a need to bolster belief in the immortality of the soul, his theology will profit only that "Christian church" where membership is based on the recitation of phrases left in studied ambiguity. Theological spokesmen of that "Christian" church will either choose to ignore a work like Jaki's, or they will write as did Sharpe: "An apology for a traditional Christian stance, especially one as vast as Jaki's, needs a more persuasive and convincing motivation than the one supplied by Jaki. In fact I do not believe Jaki's very extensive polemics will alter the course of our society and its beliefs one iota. His thought on science, for instance, is on the whole only available to scholars, and his conclusions on present and future science and society rest on grounds — namely his highly controversial comprehension of the history of science — probably not of sufficient strength to generate change."[2]

Such was an unwittingly strange admission, a point that should be obvious to anyone mindful of the gigantic measure of that change were it ever to take place. Clearly, if Jaki's arguments and scholarship carried with them the mere probability of bringing about that change, they should have been given a most careful and at least a moderately benevolent consideration, qualities absent in Sharpe's article.

At any rate, Jaki never in all his writings voiced the hope that modern society — an agnostic and hedonistic society, that is — could be shaken in its beliefs however slightly by arguments, however scholarly. As one who was not afraid to speak openly and at length of original sin, this chief target of liberal theologizing, in relation to the history of science,[3] he would consider such hope, so dear to liberals, to be a mere illusion. Clearly, there is a world of difference between the views of Jaki, who casts Christ into the non–liberal but liberating role of being the Savior of science, and those of Teilhard de Chardin, that darling of modern Catholic (and revealingly also of Protestant) liberal thought, who did his very best to draw a portrait of a cosmic Christ that had practically nothing to do with original sin. Liberal Christians — Catholics or Protestants — have little if any appreciation of Jaki's work for a simple reason. They know all too well the ecclesiology professed by Jaki who as a Christian never wanted to appear other than a *Roman* Catholic. They know that Jaki never advocated syncretism — theological, philosophical, or ethical — in any form. Apart from ecclesiology, the liberals' studiedly vague idea of the Christian church and life would, when exposed to Jaki's message, have the fate similar to that of fluffy clouds whenever hit by steady sunlight. No wonder that they did their very best to blunt the impact of the Templeton Prize accorded to Jaki by characterizing the award as "the most controversial" in its history.[4]

Christians at the other end of the spectrum, that is, fundamentalists and revivalists, found useful Jaki's battling the reductionists, but were very much rankled by Jaki's strictures of a literal six-day creation,[5] and by his endorsements of biological evolution on grounds far more reliable than Darwinists could ever propose.[6] Furthermore, Jaki's insistence on the specifically medieval origin of science disturbed them even more than their liberal counterparts, who came to realize that the slighting of the Middle Ages is not a necessarily respectable scholarly attitude.

Quite positive has been the reception of Jaki's work in Protestant circles, steadily shrinking, where a serious effort is made to strike a course between liberalism and fundamentalism.[7] Yet even there Jaki, the Catholic theologian arguing from the perspective of science and its history and philosophy, remains, time again, a bitter pill to swallow. While some recent Catholic thinkers may not realize the consequences of accepting this or that intellectual standpoint, their Protestant counterparts are more alive in that respect. They seem to realize what is implied in Jaki's unwavering support of a natural theology which includes not only the rational demonstration of the existence of God but also that of the immortality of the soul.[8] Such natural theology rests on moderate realism's program to recognize continuity across the welter of change. Continuity is, however, the chief target of that nominalist tradition which is the philosophical justification of discontinuity between the Church of the apostles and the post-apostolic Church.[9]

Unstinting appreciation of Jaki's work came, though somewhat belatedly, from Catholic circles that are nowadays labeled traditional or conservative, though they merely hold that, to recall a phrase of Chesterton, Christianity is no longer Christian if it is not dogmatic.[10] To recall Chesterton is all the more appropriate in view of Jaki's spirited defense of the depth of Chesterton's conversion to Catholicism against some recent portrayals of him as a champion of "mere Christianity,"[11] a label for which Jaki has little use.[12] The appreciation of those Catholics of Jaki's work is best illustrated by R. V. Young's comments: "Jaki's argument that creative scientific endeavour is nurtured by the epistemology of Christian natural theology marks a new departure in the resolution of the current crisis of faith and reason, a crisis which recurs at decisive moments in the temporal life of the Church."[13] For such Catholics Jaki will continue to be of capital importance for the life of the Church in its attempts at evangelizing the scientific world.

These opinions, so widely differing in their thrust, about Jaki's work were recalled here to clear the ground for its value for the pastoral mission of the Roman Catholic Church. Jaki has declined to appear in platforms sponsored by Christian groups who claim to themselves the task of pastoral renewal while they systematically ignore the Bishops and especially the Pope.[14] The portrayal of some specific aspects of Jaki's work as given in the preceding chapter should seem detailed enough to allow for its comparison with views proposed by various organs of the pastoral office of the Church concerning the apostolate among scientists.

An appropriate starting point may be the questionnaire sent out by the Vatican Secretariat for Non-Believers (now the Pontifical Council for Dialogue with Non-Believers) to all the episcopal conferences during the years 1978-1980 about the problem of science and non-belief. One of the questions asked was: "Among the conclusions reached by contemporary science, which would you say present particular difficulties for the Faith (e.g. the origins and evolution of the universe and of man; the origin of life; man's place in the universe, etc.)?"[15] Not only have these topics received a sustained consideration in Jaki's work but they were placed within a perspective of the greatest concern to that Secretariat. The perspective is one that includes not only the highly developed countries but also the countries still in the initial phases of technologization. In the former, Jaki's work is most relevant to the endless misunderstandings, historical and philosophical, about the respective competence of science and of theology. In the latter, the survival of traditional world views (not merely organismic but also plainly animistic) is at times so strong as to call for considerations that Jaki has set forth about science and ancient cultures. His work could also greatly help Catholics in those countries to form a realistic idea about some deep-seated cultural causes of their scientific and technological backwardness which is often traced, and rather simplistically, to colonizing exploitation.

The heavily documented and scholarly argued character of Jaki's work will prevent it from becoming popular fare and a handy pastoral tool. This is not to suggest that some of his works, such as *Cosmos and Creator* and *The Savior of Science*, are not within the reach of a non-specialist readership. His message should, however, be first absorbed by this nowadays especially-fragmented group called Catholic intellectuals, if it is ever to filter down to a suitable fraction of the Catholic, to say nothing of the Christian, public at large. Those who claim that Jaki's "polemical style" prevents his work from being accepted widely, should consider whether by cultivating a "non-polemic" style, they may not be engaged in a polemic aimed at creating the illusion that almost all views are equally good. And when a liberal Protestant, such as F. Ferré, makes that charge about Jaki's "polemical" style,[16] one may be rightly suspicious. Is he not pleading for that sole certainty which is to feel firmly uncertain about any religious truth? Polemics, or at least a touch of it, is inseparable from facing up openly to the relation of one's position to positions very different from it.

Those who appreciate that kind of frankness, will find in Jaki's work not a "simplistic apologetics" but an openness based on a true metaphysical vision.[17] They may take comfort in the fact that Jaki's work received the highest endorsement on the part of some who are very distant from the Christian, let alone from the Catholic position. Regarding *Brain, Mind and Computers* H. Feigl wrote: "Rev. Dr. Jaki presents a sustained, well-informed and persuasive argument for mind-body dualism. . . . My own prejudices and predilections are exactly opposite to Dr. Jaki's conclusions, but I welcome his challenge — it deserves to be taken seriously — and to be answered."[18] A letter from K. R. Popper to Jaki contains this admission: "Let me tell you that I am most impressed by your writings (so far as I know them); I am not a historian of science, but it seems to me that you are not only an extremely competent historian of science but also an outstanding philosopher of science. Your criticism of my views on Kant's cosmology are very fair and probably right."[19] These remarks from two prominent philosophers of science may give second thoughts to some Christians and Catholics about their tardiness in discovering Jaki's work.

That work should seem of the greatest relevance in view of some highly noted studies concerning pastoral work in a world of science, a world that has, as F. Russo wrote, "become increasingly secularized since the end of the 18th century."[20] This secularization has received much added momentum from a positivist interpretation of science. While this has been well aired, little has been offered, apart from Jaki's work about the gradual turning of the scientific enterprise against the very Christian matrix which assured its first viable birth. It is not a process to do scholarly or moral credit to its promoters. And Jaki minces no words. From the Encyclopedists and Comte onwards, he wrote, there developed "that modern parasitism which with its pseudo-sophistication lives off the Christian cultural heritage and scorns it at the same time."[21] Jaki's historical approach should greatly help Christians and Catholics to overcome an inferiority complex in viewing the relation between faith and science. His work could also greatly help them to avoid the pitfall of developing a false sense of superiority which is bred by the cultivation of facile concordism between those two fields. In Jaki's portrayal of the methods of those two fields, they are always kept separate in order to be correlated in a realist perspective.

Russo's reflections on the secularization of science contain a reference to modern efforts aimed at coping, with the help of science, with the question of the origin of the world: "The increasingly plausible hypothesis according to which the universe initially came into being at a time in which matter was extremely concentrated is, without any doubt, a purely scientific question. Philosophers are quite right to maintain that the notion of creation is something which lies beyond this purely scientific aspect of the question. Nevertheless, this 'coming into being' of the universe is a problem both for philosophy and religious thought."[22] As we have seen, Jaki is careful not to confuse the philosophical or theological notion of the beginning of the cosmos with the provisionally last frontier of cosmological research. Nor is he condoning the claims of some cosmologists that science might answer the question about the absolute origin of the universe. Instead of speaking, as Russo does, of a continuity and discontinuity between science and theology concerning that origin, Jaki emphasizes the invariable specificity of scientific findings about the universe. He does not rely on science to unfold the philosophical and theological significance of those specificities, so many marks of the contingency of the universe.

Russo also voiced the hope that those who work in the evangelization and pastoral care of the scientific community "will take their inspiration first and foremost from the teaching of the Church in this regard, for it is not sufficiently well known, even though it provides the most reliable and sound bases."[23] Undoubtedly, there is no Catholic historian and philosopher of science whose writings have been more explicit on matters theological. A look at the extent to which Jaki has been inspired by the teaching of the Church in these matters and is in accord with it will now be considered.

The teaching office of the Church

Theology, even when indirectly taken up as all too often the case in Jaki's writings on the history and philosophy of science, is part of the life of the community of the faithful. It must therefore be at the service of faith and in conformity with the teaching office of the Church.[24] That office is rooted in Peter's successor who is "the perpetual and visible source and foundation of unity both of the bishops and of the whole company of the faithful."[25] The fact that he is a source conveys his dynamic role, which is to maintain the unity in an ever changing ecclesial world. The Church changes because it is in a world of change, a point which Newman had put tersely as he portrayed the kind of doctrinal development that remains faithful to its type: "To live is to change and to change often."[26] The Pope therefore has to address himself to that principal source of change in modern life, which is science. Its relation to faith is a symptom which, whatever its sameness in some essentials, always presents new aspects. Moreover the changes are global and therefore they call particularly for the attention of the papacy, the sole individually global pastoral office in the Church.

Jaki's loyalty to the Church and its magisterium is very evident from his works, especially those dedicated to ecclesiology.[27] The reverse side of that loyalty is his readiness to be inspired by the living magisterium. Early in his career he derived much inspiration from various addresses of Pius XII to the Pontifical Academy of Sciences and in particular from the Pope's discourse of November 22, 1951, on the proofs of the existence of God in the light of modern science.[28] In fact, that address him gave the idea, several years before he started his graduate training in physics, to work out eventually a proof of creation in time on the basis of entropy. By the time he had received his Ph.D. in physics, Jaki realized that such a proof was impossible. As he grew also more familiar with the works of E. T. Whittaker, the chief advisor of Pius XII in matters scientific, he began to see the Pope's carefulness in drawing the conclusion: "Indeed, it seems that the science of today, by going back in one leap millions of centuries, has succeeded in being a witness to that primordial Fiat Lux, when, out of nothing, there burst forth with matter a sea of light and radiation, while the particles of chemical elements split and reunited in millions of galaxies."[29]

The Pope's care was all the more noteworthy as he quoted a passage from Whittaker's Donnellan Lectures which suggested that science could somehow spot the moment of creation: "Different estimates converge to the conclusion that there was an epoch about 10^9 or 10^{10} years ago, on the further side of which the cosmos, if it existed at all, existed in some form totally different from anything known to us: so that it represents the ultimate limit of science. We may perhaps without impropriety refer to it as the Creation."[30] Pius

XII, as Jaki noted, was careful to claim for metaphysics and theology any reference to creation proper. Such a concern was, according to Jaki, all the more creditable as Whittaker's reading of the science of the moment was not unobjectionable. In this context Jaki listed such facts as the disagreement at that time between the estimated age of the earth and the past duration of the expansion of the universe. Also, it could not be proven that the rate of expansion has always been constant. Moreover, there could have existed a state of matter before the expansion started, a state not accessible to the present form of science. The Pope was therefore in a sense defended against Whittaker when Jaki wrote that it was "dangerous to consider the actual state of scientific research as the ultimate word," for "scientific explanations are by no means exhaustive, nor can one take it for granted that all the physical forces are known to science today."[31]

The same defense was continued as Jaki wrote: "The pope's speech stressed that the data reviewed still needed further research, that they were in need of further development before they could provide a sure foundation for philosophical arguments, that the scientific answer in question was neither explicit nor complete."[32] Indeed, the Pope made it clear that science, which has nothing to do with creation out of nothing, could not even demonstrate creation in time. Jaki further quoted the Pope to the effect that such demonstrations ought to be drawn from "metaphysics and revelation, in so far as they concern creation in its widest sense, and from revelation alone in so far as they concern creation in time" and that "creation itself lies outside the sphere of the natural sciences."[33]

That there is need for such defense of papal allocutions on science received further proof in Hawking's rude distortion of what Pius XII had said about the expansion of the universe. Hawking must have had in mind the Pope's 1951 allocution to the Pontifical Academy of Sciences in stating that "the Catholic Church . . . seized on the big bang model and in 1951 officially pronounced it to be in accord with the Bible."[34] Jaki was the only Catholic writer to call attention to this rank distortion of facts which, as he warned, is now creating another historic lie about the Catholic Church owing to the millions of copies sold of Hawking's book. It is indeed a sad reflection on our secularist culture that, as Jaki notes in the same context, applauds scientists who try to step in the Creator' shoes as they are busy "evicting the Creator."[35]

Undoubtedly, more than one exception could be made to the over-enthusiastic tone of the Pope's speech. In fact, as Jaki pointed out, distinctly different was the tone of the Pope's subsequent speech on much the same subject to a gathering of astronomers.[36] There, as if to balance his earlier statement, the Pope dwelt on the difference between the methods of science and that of philosophy and theology. Implied in that difference is the respective autonomy of those various fields of inquiry. That difference found a noteworthy expression in the teaching of Vatican II: "By the very nature of creation, material being is endowed with its own stability, truth and excellence, its own order and laws. These man must respect as he recognizes the methods proper to every science and technique." This autonomy is not, of course, to be understood as if the material world had an existence on its own, for "without a creator there can be no creature."[37]

At any rate, this teaching of Vatican II is a very recent link in a long and distinctly Catholic theological and philosophical tradition. Jaki notes that "already at the dawn of the medieval grappling with the relation of reason and revelation explicit statements were made . . . on behalf of the impersonal and autonomous character of the laws of nature."[38] He also remarks that conflicts between science and theology started when an a priori truth was assigned to the autonomy of science. The inability of science to spot the moment of creation, whether on the basis of Big Bang or any other other basis, is merely one of many of such inabilities of science to deal with metaphysical, theological and ethical questions patently outside its competence. Only through paying attention to the limitedness of the scientific method can one avoid the pitfalls of scientism, points argued by Jaki time and again.[39]

He began to argue those points at great length from the mid-1960's on, the early years of the pontificate of Paul VI who repeatedly touched upon them. The ecclesial nature of the work of Jaki, whose writings on the history and philosophy of science contain no reference to Paul VI, will appear in bold relief against a brief recall of some of the points the Pope made. Paul VI called attention to the limitations of the scientific method in asking: "Does it exhaust the whole of reality, or is it not rather a mere segment, the one pertaining to the truths that can be reached by scientific processes?"[40] The fact that it does not, will not, as the Pope warned two years later, isolate science from metaphysics, for "science prepares for and presupposes an order of thought which transcends and justifies it."[41] Concerning the metaphysical order, Pope Paul VI in the introduction to his *Credo of the People of God* reiterated a principle which is fundamental to science as well as to a metaphysics and epistemology based on Christian belief in God the Creator: "It is of the greatest importance to recognize that over and above what is visible, the reality of which we discern through the sciences, God has given us an intellect which can attain to *that which* is not merely the subjective content of the 'structures' and developments of human consciousness."[42]

This last statement, which strikes at the heart of Kantian subjectivism, may indeed serve as an indirect approval of Jaki's relentless criticism of Kant as an interpreter of science. As to the statement of Paul VI that man must never stop at physical reality but must go beyond it to him who is the Source of all, the one necessary Being, to the Creator[43] — this is obviously the chief thrust of Jaki's work. He is the only major Catholic philosopher and historian of science who extensively investigated the epistemology of the cosmological argument as an epistemology most germane to creative science. He alone, in that framework, made a detailed study of the role which Revelation about creation played in strengthening natural reason in articulating that argument, without endorsing even a touch of fideism as he wrote as the grand conclusion of his *Cosmos and Creator.* "In a very crucial sense, one must first say Creator in order to say Cosmos." By this he meant that it is not so much cosmology or philosophy that propels man's ideology, but much rather the great facts of salvation history. For Jaki the reality of the cosmos remains "the indispensable stepping stone for a rational recognition of the existence of the Creator."[44]

The ecclesial character of Jaki's thinking, which contains so much on the specificity of the cosmos, will stand again in bold relief when taken against one of Paul VI's last major addresses on these matters. In that address, given on February 9, 1977, the Pope spoke of the material world as a pointer towards God. He rejected reflections on that world in which it is left without ultimate explanation, or is turned into a self-explanatory system, let alone when given "divine" qualities in line with pantheism. The pope contrasted the false approaches to the reality of the world with that of genuine science which invariably asks, "Why is the world so?" and gives but a specifically limited answer to that question.[45]

To turn now to the teaching given by John Paul II on these matters is justified for more than one reason. One is that this Pope spoke more often and in far greater detail than all previous Popes. Also the second main phase of Jaki's work largely coincides with the present pontificate during which his work received an indirect approbation through his being named, as an historian and philosopher of science, an honorary member of the Pontifical Academy of Sciences. Four themes stand out in the Pope's teaching relating to these matters. One relates to the incomplete nature of science, or rather to the limitedness of its method. Another deals with the cosmos as a strict unity. The third is about the unique rise of science. The fourth has the dogma of creation for its object. Again, the fact that Jaki never quoted John Paul II on these topics should reveal the instinctively ecclesial character of Jaki's discussion of them as they form the main aspects of his work.

The incomplete nature of science

In his historic address, delivered in Cologne Cathedral on November 15, 1980, Pope John Paul II first noted in general the limits of science: "Scientific affirmations are always particular. They are justified only in consideration of a given starting point, they are set in a process of development, and they can be corrected and left behind in this process." He then pointed at the conviction that the world is orderly and brought into focus the principal aspect of the limitedness of science by asking: "But above all: how could something constitute the result of a scientific starting point when it first justifies this starting point and therefore must already be presupposed by it?"[46] A year later the Pope restated before the Pontifical Academy of Sciences that science is limited in itself, for "the conquests of science are at times provisional, subject to review and rethinking, and they will never succeed in expressing the whole truth hidden in the Universe." The same science appeared also limited in relation to other disciplines as the Pope continued about "truths which science cannot discover, but which question the mind of the scientist in the innermost part of his being, where he experiences an irresistible longing and yearning for the divine."[47]

While these points have always been central in Jaki's writings he also emphasized one specific point, not touched upon by the Pope. The point relates to what is to be meant by the total explanation science can give. Jaki kept saying that it is possible for science to give eventually a total account of the quantitative aspects of material things. A further aspect of this claim of Jaki's is that even when science succeeds in doing so, it can never be sure, either theoretically or empirically, that it has reached that final account.[48] Also, Jaki has always stressed that the account is not an explanation in the ontological sense which the Pope clearly had in mind in saying that science "will never succeed in expressing the whole truth hidden in the Universe."

The Pope has also applied this understanding of the incompleteness of science to the discussion of the proofs of the existence of God: "To desire a scientific proof of God would be equivalent to lowering God to the level of the beings of our world, and we would therefore be mistaken methodologically in regard to what God is. Science must recognize its limits and its inability to reach the existence of God: it can neither affirm nor deny his existence."[49] In particular, the Pope has urged the utmost caution concerning the use of the big-bang theory as a means of arriving at a notion of creation in time: "Any scientific hypothesis on the origin of the world, such as the hypothesis of a primitive atom from which derived the whole of the physical universe, leaves open the problem concerning the universe's beginning. Science cannot of itself solve this question: there is needed that human knowledge that rises above physics and astrophysics and which is called metaphysics; there is needed above all the knowledge that comes from God's revelation."[50] John Paul II made it clear that metaphysics and revelation are needed in any discussion of the origin of the cosmos. The consonance of Jaki's views and arguments on these matters with the papal teaching should be all too obvious. What he adds as his contribution, apart from a few specific theoretical arguments, is a wealth of data and views from the history and philosophy of science, remote and recent. Much the same is true concerning the next topic.

The cosmos as unity

The originality of Jaki's definition of the cosmos as the totality of consistently and most specifically interacting things, a definition as useful for metaphysics as for physical science, has already been noted several times in the foregoing pages.[51] In a more general sense the same has been repeatedly emphasized by Pope John Paul II. His address, of December 22, 1980, to Nobel Prize winners contains the following phrase: "The believer holds that the world has an explanation and that, as science advances arduously and toilsomely, even if at times it hesitates and loses its way, it must reach an understanding that the universe constitutes = as the very etymology of the word 'universe' indicates = a complex order in which the various elements are harmoniously related with one another."[52] On another occasion, the Pope stressed the need of the universe, taken as a totality of all beings, to be related to its ultimate ground: "The ensemble of creatures *constitutes the universe*: the visible and invisible cosmos, in the totality and the parts of which *there is reflected eternal Wisdom* and expressed the inexhaustible *Love of the Creator.*"[53]

Jaki's insistence on epistemological realism and his strictures of cosmologists who have increasingly taken their mathematical formalisms for so many sources of physical reality, including that of the universe itself, has a parallel in some momentous warnings made by John Paul II. He seized the opportunity of a study week promoted by the Vatican Observatory to remind its participants that "man is created *one* in his different capabilities to know the real: whether they be analytical or synthetical, inductive or deductive, observational or intuitive." From this it followed, the Pope went on, that the cosmos as the object of knowledge "must not be manipulated nor reduced a priori to a mathematical model, but must include the totality of the real."[54] Such warnings must be heeded by the scientific community before they can be assumed to be willing to steer clear of scientism. The latter in its cosmic dimensions was the target of the Pope's admonition that science "cannot close itself to the *universal*, nor to the knowledge of things as a whole, nor to the *Absolute*, even if it is unable by itself to answer the question of meaning."[55]

The unique rise of science

The many addresses given by John Paul II on science do not contain explicit mention of the unique rise of science as sparked by the medievals' coming to grips with the difference between Aristotelian pantheism and the stipulations of the Faith concerning the origin of the universe. This point, so central in Jaki's reflections, is, however, implicitly present in the Pope's various discourses on related matters. One such discourse of the Pope was the one he delivered to scientists and students in Cologne. There, as he extolled the work of Albertus

Magnus, a glory of the medieval university of Cologne, he spoke of him as one who struck a wise middle course between two extremes. One was to ignore novel information which at that time was Aristotle's philosophy and natural science (mediated through the Arabs), the other a wholesale surrender to the novelty.[56] Another intimation by the Pope of the medieval matrix of modern science can be found in his address of 1981 to the Pontifical Academy of Sciences. There he called attention to the scriptural vision of the world, a vision that taught man to explore the world: "The Sacred Book likewise wishes to tell men that the world was not created as the seat of the gods, as was taught by other cosmogonies and cosmologies, but was rather created for the service of man and the glory of God. Any other teaching about the origin and make-up of the universe is alien to the intentions of the Bible, which does not wish to teach how heaven was made but how one goes to heaven."[57]

Without bringing in that medieval matrix, the Pope gave, in early January 1986, much credit to the biblical vision of the world about the origin of science: "It may be said that the roots of modern science are closely linked to the biblical truth about creation, even though the relationship between the two has not always been harmonious."[58]   A week later, again in a General Audience, the Pope referred to Saint Paul's speech on the   Areopagus as an introduction to his remarks on the universality of natural theology: "It is interesting that the Athenians, who recognized many gods (pagan polytheism), should have heard these words on the one God, the Creator, without raising objection. This fact seems to confirm that the truth about creation constitutes a meeting-point between those who profess different religions. Perhaps the truth about creation is rooted in an innate and fundamental way in diverse religions, even if they have not sufficiently clear concepts, such as those contained in the Sacred Scriptures."[59]

The light which Biblical Revelation can provide for a proper interpretation of the rudiments of a creation doctrine in non-monotheistic religions, has been the object of many theological studies. Few Christian theologians have been eager to note a most healthy effect of science on religious cultures, including those formed by monotheistic and Christian religions. The effect is the discrediting of superstitious practices and miracle mongering. Jaki is one of these theologians, and in fact one of the very few, who also called attention to the debt which science owes to Christian religion. It is a similar balance that has been held high by the Pope as he declared: "Science can purify religion from error and superstition; religion can purify science from idolatry and false absolutes."[60]

The dogma of creation

The frequent returns of Jaki to various aspects of the dogma of creation and to its first major document, Genesis 1,[61] have, apart from their rich details, a general tone which is most consonant with various utterances of John Paul II. As regards the creation accounts of Genesis, the Pope made it clear that notwithstanding the similarities between the cosmogonies of the time and the discourse of the inspired author, the latter "inserts with absolute originality the truth about the creation of everything by the one God: this is the revealed truth." The created character of all implies its being created out of nothing, a point which the Pope felt necessary to emphasize by calling attention to the brazenly heretical character of its denial: "It is . . . contrary to faith to deny that the world and all things contained therein, whether spiritual or material, in their entire substance have been created by God out of nothing."[62] In addition to referring to solemn declarations of this point at Lateran IV and Vatican I, the Pope also referred to Tradition: "The Fathers of the Church and theologians clarified further the meaning of the divine action by speaking of creation 'from nothing'."[63] The Pope thought it equally important to stress the dogmatic character of the age-old teaching of the Church about creation in time: "the world was created by God in time, therefore, it is not eternal: it has a beginning in time."[64] Jaki was certainly not one of those Catholic philosophers of science, who, in spite of their theological training as priests, found nothing contrary to faith in the steady-state theory or in some cosmologists' claims about the factual eternity of the world, let alone in their claim that they are able to create literally entire universes out of nothing.

Jaki's repeated insistence on the dogma of creation as the basis of the whole Creed and the ground of all other dogmas about the work of salvation, finds full justification in John Paul II's declaration: "We should, however, recall that the order of salvation not only presupposes creation, but indeed originates from it. The Creed, in its conciseness, refers us back to the *ensemble of revealed truth about creation*, to discover the truly singular and eminent position granted to man."[65] Much the same can be said in reference to the Pope's insistence that, for the future good of humanity, belief in God the Creator must once again link up with science, philosophy, theology and other aspects of life: One of the major cultural tasks of our time is, to quote the Pope, that of "integrating knowledge, in the sense of a synthesis, in which the impressive body of scientific knowledge may find its meaning within the framework of an integral vision of man and of the universe."[66] It is precisely that monumental synthesis concerning Christian belief in God the Creator, philosophy, science, history and culture which Jaki has achieved.

Jaki's work has shown how Christian belief in God the Creator has been, through philosophical reflections on it, the stimulus which nurtured the birth of modern science in its medieval cradle. The rational grounds of that faith are corroborated by the stark specificity uncovered by modern science about the universe. The moral consequences of this faith in God the Creator are crucial for the present and future application of science and technology. In view of this, Catholic intellectuals, but especially theologians, would do well to acquire a thorough familiarity with Jaki's works. They constitute a pivotal tool — historical, philosophical, and theological — in the great task of turning science into a blessing, natural as well as supernatural, for humanity.

Jaki's vision could also very well have an important role regarding ecumenical dialogue. The condition of this is, however, the measure in which theologians would realize that all denominational differences touch upon the dogma of creation, and in fact are a derivative of the meaning attached to that dogma. Attention to Jaki's work would help free that dialogue from initial ambiguities. His work may also help in restoring respectability to metaphysical realism. Since the latter, as Jaki showed, can alone cope with science, it should also regain its erstwhile status in theology which, as its history has shown again and again, relies on epistemology at every step. Reflections on Jaki's manifold message would also help theology to seek its "scientific" status in directions that have much to do with real science and its real history. Further, only when there is a meeting of minds on creation can one hope for an agreement in less broad but still very philosophical points involved in the doctrine of Incarnation, real presence, grace and free will, and the nature and structure of the

Church. The well being of all Christians and indeed of all humanity depends on a Church that, in this age of science, grasps the full breadth and depth of its belief in "one God, the Father Almighty, the Creator of Heaven and Earth, of all things visible and invisible."

NOTES

Introduction

[1] Pope John Paul II, "Address to Twelve Nobel Prize-Winners," Dec. 22, 1980, in *Insegnamenti di Giovanni Paolo II* (Vatican Polyglot Press, 1978 -), 3/2 (1980), p. 1784. Cardinal Ratzinger has also noted that insufficient attention seems to be given today to the doctrine of the creation: "This happens, too, because one fears the problems (and accordingly would like to avoid them) posed by the relationship between faith in creation and the natural sciences." J. Cardinal Ratzinger and V. Messori, *The Ratzinger Report* (Leominster, England: Fowler Wright Books, 1985), p. 78.

[2] K. Baker, "Creator of Heaven and Earth," in *Homiletic and Pastoral Review* 84 (December 1983), p. 80.

[3] See Second Vatican Council, *Gaudium et Spes* 33.2 in *Acta Apostolicae Sedis* 58 (1966), p. 1052.

[4] See First Vatican Council, Dogmatic Constitution *Dei Filius* on the Catholic Faith, ch. 4, Concerning Faith and Reason: "nulla tamen umquam inter fidem et rationem vera dissensio esse potest." See H. Denzinger and A. Schönmetzer, *Enchiridion Symbolorum* (Roma: Herder, 1976), #3017 (henceforth referred to as DS).

[5] E. Bellone in *Scientia: Rivista di Scienza*, 112 (1977), p. 842.

[6] *And on This Rock* 1978(4), p. 13.

Chapter One

[1] See 1957(1) and 1963(1). I was present when at a chance meeting of Cardinal Ratzinger and Father Jaki at the Collegio Pontificio Portoghese in September 1987, His Eminence quickly turned the conversation to Jaki's *Tendances nouvelles* with the remark: "It occupies a place of honor in my library."

[2] Personal communication from S. L. Jaki.

[3] Delivered on Feb. 21, 1943 and Nov. 22, 1951, respectively.

[4] See "The Teacher: Dr. Victor Hess. The Student: Rev. Stanley Jaki," 1985(13).

[5] See 1958(1).

[6] See the fourteen items with a Hungarian title listed between 1958 and 1965.

[7] University of Chicago Press, unpublished letter to S. L. Jaki, of October 20, 1965.

[8] W. Heitler, "Essay Review on *The Relevance of Physics,*" *American Scientist* 55 (1967), p. 352.

[9] "Brain, Mind and Computers," 1972(7), p. 12.

[10] See his acceptance speech, 1972(2).

[11] *1987 Templeton Prize* (Nassau, Bahamas: Lismore Press, 1987), p. 4.

[12] See 1983(6) and 1985(7).

[13] From the text in the Archives of the Pontifical Academy of Sciences, to be published in full in the Proceedings of its Plenary Session of 1990.

[14] H. Duhem, *Un savant français. Pierre Duhem* (Paris: Plon, 1936).

[15] Such as *Prémices philosophiques* 1987(3) and *The Physicist as Artist: The Landscapes of Pierre Duhem* 1988(3).

[16] See 1984(1) and 1987(2).

[17] *Pierre Duhem: Scientist and Catholic* (Front Royal, Va.: Christendom Press, 1991) and its French translation by F. Raymondaud, *Pierre Duhem: Homme de foi et de science* (Paris: Beauchesne, 1991).

[18] *Science and Creation* 1974(1), 1986(1) and 1990(7).

[19] At his urging, Philip Trower translated Gilson's epistemological treatise, *Le réalisme méthodique* (1936), into English, *Methodical Realism* (Front Royal, Va: Christendom Press, 1990) with an introduction by Jaki.

[20] See *Chesterton: A Seer of Science* 1986(4).

[21] See "Maritain and Science" 1984(2).

[22] 1978(4) and 1987(1).

[23] 1986(3).

Chapter Two

[1] Jaki's use of the word "phenomenology" is not overburdened with the specious distinctions of which an overview can be gained by a perusal of K. Lehmann, "Phenomenology," in K. Rahner (ed.), *Encyclopaedia of Theology (The Concise Sacramentum Mundi)* (New York: The Seabury Press, 1975), pp. 1225-1228.

[2] See *The Relevance of Physics* 1966(1), p. 532 and "God and Man's Science" 1984(4), pp. 36-39.

[3] *The Road of Science and the Ways to God* 1978(2), p. 326.

[4] *The Relevance of Physics* 1966(1), pp. 507-14.

[5] "The Last Century of Science" 1973(4), pp. 250-51.

[6] Ibid., p. 254-55. See also "Science and Christian Theism" 1979(7), p. 563, where Jaki states that "science is a self-sustaining enterprise which feeds on its own successes and in a measure that seems to surpass even the fertility of geometrical progression."

[7] "The Last Century of Science" 1973(4), p. 260.

[8] *The Relevance of Physics* 1966(1), pp. 137 and 274.

[9] See *The Road of Science and the Ways to God* 1978(2), p. 85, where Jaki states that Newton would have had "no use for that outlook in which the objective truth of a given explanatory device, or hypothesis was as much — or rather as little — as that of any other hypothesis."

[10] *The Relevance of Physics* 1966(1), p. 390.

[11] *The Road of Science and the Ways to God* 1978(2), pp. 308-09.

[12] *The Relevance of Physics* 1966(1), ch. 13, *God and the Cosmologists* 1989(1), p. 79, and *The Road of Science and the Ways to God* 1978(2) p. 308.

[13] "The Last Century of Science" 1973(4), pp. 259-63.

[14] See *The Relevance of Physics* 1966(1), p. 505.

[15] Ibid., p. 499.

[16] *The Road of Science and the Ways to God* 1978(2), p. 237.

[17] Ibid., pp. 232-44, 420-24; see also *Cosmos and Creator* 1980(1), p. 97.

[18] *The Relevance of Physics* 1966(1), pp. 405 and 505. Jaki refers to H. Poincaré, "La morale et la science," in *Dernières pensées* (Paris: Flammarion, 1913), p. 241.

[19] "Goethe and the Physicists" 1969(3); "De la science-fiction à la philosophie" 1981(4), p. 42; see also *The Road of Science and the Ways to God* 1978(2), p. 107.

[20] *The Relevance of Physics* 1966(1), p. 502.

[21] Ibid., pp. 519 and 533.

[22] *Culture and Science* 1975(5), pp. 15 and 19-20. Jaki's references are to C. P. Snow, *The Two Cultures and a Second Look* (Cambridge: University Press, 1969).

[23] *The Relevance of Physics* 1966(1), p. 515.

[24] Ibid., pp. 373, 466, 495.

[25] Ibid., p. 516.

[26] *The Relevance of Physics* 1966(1), ch. 1 and *Science and Creation* 1974(1), chs. 1-6, and 9.

[27] *The Road of Science and the Ways to God* 1978(2), p. 20.

[28] "The Greeks of Old and the Novelty of Science" 1983(5), p. 276.

[29] *The Relevance of Physics* 1966(1), pp. 50-52.

[30] Ibid., pp. 91 and 94.

[31] Ibid., ch. 3, "The World as a Pattern in Numbers."

[32] Ibid., pp. 121 and 124.

[33] Ibid., pp. 127-30.

[34] *Cosmos and Creator* 1980(1), p. 49.

[35] *God and the Cosmologists* 1989(1), p. 106 and *The Savior of Science* 1988(1), p. 109.

[36] *Cosmos and Creator* 1980(1), p. 51.

[37] *The Relevance of Physics* 1966(1), pp. 130 and 137.

[38] Ibid., p. 141.

[39] Ibid., pp. 187 and 137.

[40] "Physics and the Ultimate" 1988(8), pp. 63-64.

[41] See *The Paradox of Olbers' Paradox* 1969(2), *The Milky Way: An Elusive Road for Science* 1975(2), *Planets and Planetarians* 1978(1) and his translations, with notes and introduction of works by Giordano Bruno, Lambert, and Kant.

[42] *The Relevance of Physics* 1966(1), pp. 207 and 216.

[43] The theme of ch. 8 in *The Milky Way* 1972(1).

[44] This latter claim is implied in the steady-state theory, a point which only Jaki has noted so far among the critics of that theory. For his latest criticism of the steady state theory, see his *God and the Cosmologists*, ch. 5.

[45] See *God and the Cosmologists* 1990(1), p. 81.

[46] *The Relevance of Physics* 1966(1), pp. 236 and 265-73. See Chapter Three below on Jaki's critique of the prevailing interpretation of the uncertainty principle.

[47] Ibid., p. 501. This error of scientism is, as Jaki notes, also damaging to other spheres of human activity: "By setting quantitative exactitude as the only and supreme test of truth, scientism robs of meaning the world of qualities and values," *Chesterton. A Seer of Science* 1986(4), p. 50.

[48] *Culture and Science* 1975(5), pp. 45-47. See also "On Whose Side Is History?" 1985(6), p. 46, where Jaki states that "scientists, however, rarely remind themselves that their language — the language of quantities — is a very limited language; and much less do they trouble themselves to recall that the origin of that language is a broadly shared vision of the whole material world as the embodiment of quantities."

[49] See *The Relevance of Physics* 1966(1), pp. 434-37.

[50] Ibid., p. 513.

[51] *The Road of Science and the Ways to God* 1978(2), p. 64.

⁵² Ibid., p. 152.

⁵³ See ibid., ch. 14, entirely devoted to the "ravages of reductionism" as the fruits of logical positivism.

⁵⁴ See ibid., ch. 15, "Paradigms or Paradigm," the second half of which consists of Jaki's criticism of the illogicalities of Kuhn's notion of paradigms and of his mishandling of the facts of the history of science.

⁵⁵ *Cosmos and Creator*, 1980(1), p. 89.

⁵⁶ In *The Road of Science and the Ways to God* 1978(2), pp. 76-77, Jaki rightly makes much of Spinoza's inability to cope with the objection that on the basis of his philosophy particular things cannot exist.

⁵⁷ See Introduction to his translation of Immanuel Kant *Universal Natural History and Theory of the Heavens* 1981(1), p. 71. There Jaki also expresses his hope that this translation will be helpful in showing that "the apriorism (and subjectivism) of the *Critique* is already raising its bewitching head in the *Allgemeine Naturgeschichte*" (p. 70).

⁵⁸ Both in *The Relevance of Physics* 1966(1), pp. 45-49, and *The Road of Science and the Ways to God* 1978(2), pp. 132-39.

⁵⁹ *The Road of Science and the Ways to God* 1978(2), p. 252.

⁶⁰ See ibid., where Jaki speaks of "a middle course between nominalism, in which no two valid notions can overlap ever so slightly, and idealism, in which the overlapping of all is well-nigh complete" (p. 242). A more detailed discussion of Jaki's realist position will be given in Chapter Seven.

⁶¹ See ibid., chs. 6, 11, and 12, dealing respectively with those three great creative scientists.

Chapter Three

¹ *The Road of Science and the Ways to God* 1978(2), p. 319.

[2] "The Last Century of Science" 1973(4), p. 259. See also chapters 1-6 and 9 of *Science and Creation* 1974(1).

[3] "The History of Science and the Idea of an Oscillating Universe" 1984(9), p. 140.

[4] *The Savior of Science* 1988(1), p. 30.

[5] "The History of Science and the Idea of an Oscillating Universe" 1984(9), p. 141.

[6] *Science and Creation* 1974(1), p. 14.

[7] Ibid., pp. 92-94. See also *Cosmos and Creator* 1980(1), pp. 62-65, and Chapter Four below, for a comparison between the creation story in the Old Testament and Babylonian cosmology.

[8] "The Greeks of Old and the Novelty of Science" 1983(5), p. 267.

[9] "The History of Science and the Idea of an Oscillating Universe" 1984(9), p. 243.

[10] *Science and Creation* 1974(1), p. 118.

[11] "The History of Science and the Idea of an Oscillating Universe" 1984(9), p. 144.

[12] *Science and Creation* 1974(1), p. 130.

[13] "Science and Christian Theism" 1979(7), p. 567.

[14] The divinity of the Logos proved to be a major safeguard within orthodox Christianity against the lure of pantheism, a theme set forth by Jaki in *The Savior of Science* 1988(1) and in the essay, "Christology and the Birth of Science," 1990(12).

[15] "The Physics of Impetus and the Impetus of the Koran" 1985(7), p. 157.

[16] "On Whose Side Is History?" 1985(6), pp. 43-44.

[17] A preliminary report on the scandalous factors causing that delay was given by Jaki in "Science and Censorship: Hélène Duhem and the Publication of the *Système du monde*," 1986(14).

[18] See *Pierre Duhem: Homme de foi et de science* 1991(2), pp. 129-46.

[19] *Science and Creation* 1974(1), pp. 229-30.

[20] Ibid., p. 237.

[21] *Cosmos and Creator* 1980(1), p. 80.

[22] Ibid. See also *The Road of Science and the Ways to God* 1978(2), pp. 40-43.

[23] *The Road of Science and the Ways to God* 1978(2), p. 42.

[24] Ibid., p. 38.

[25] See *Science and Creation* 1974(1), pp. 248-50. In *The Road of Science and the Ways to God* 1978(2), p. 48, Jaki states that the Renaissance was not, in many ways, conducive to the growth of science: "Astrology, magic, cabbala, and skepticism, of which Renaissance literature had an unusually large share, were as many illusory stars to lure the fragile ship of science into deadly shallows and to prevent it from reaching waters sufficiently deep for clear sailing and real advance."

[26] See *The Ash Wednesday Supper* 1975(1) pp. 22-23; Jaki was the first to translate this work of Giordano Bruno into English.

[27] *The Relevance of Physics* 1966(1), pp. 45-50.

[28] *Science and Creation* 1974(1), p. 268.

[29] See *Uneasy Genius* 1984(1), pp. 394-95, 413-14, 426-28, "God and Man's Science" 1984(1), p. 42, and *The Savior of Science* 1988(1), pp. 47-50, where Jaki traces the debt of Newton and Galileo to Buridan and Oresme.

[30] See *The Road of Science and the Ways to God* 1978(2), ch. 6, "Instinctive Middle," especially p. 87, where Jaki states: "The middle road to which

Newton was driven back again and again by his scientific creativity was
of a piece with his explicit conviction about the validity of going
mentally from the realm of phenomena to the existence of God."

[31] "God and Creation," 1973(1), p. 117.

[32] See Kant, *Universal Natural History and Theory of the Heavens* 1981(1),
pp. 33-34.

[33] Especially in the *Opus postumum*, discussed by Jaki in *The Road of
Science and the Ways to God* 1978(2), pp. 125-27.

[34] "The History of Science and the Idea of an Oscillating Universe"
1984(9), p. 148.

[35] See *Science and Creation* 1974(1), pp. 319-30.

[36] "The History of Science and the Idea of an Oscillating Universe"
1984(9), p. 145. and *Science and Creation* 1974(1), p. 131.

[37] "The Physics of Impetus and the Impetus of the Koran" 1985(7) p.
159.

[38] See "Science and Christian Theism" 1979(9), p. 565, where Jaki states:
"If it was true that every bit of matter was living and shared in the
unconscious striving of the whole, a depersonalized view of matter or a
purely quantitative handling of it could hardly have any appeal."

[39] "The History of Science and the Idea of an Oscillating Universe"
1984(9), p. 153.

[40] See *Science and Creation* 1974(1), pp. 19 and 53.

[41] *The Road of Science and the Ways to God* 1978(2), pp. 37-38.

[42] *"Physics and the Ultimate"* 1988(8), p. 65. Jaki began his critique of the
Copenhagen interpretation of Heisenberg's uncertainty principle in
"Chance or Reality" 1981(3) and developed it in full in *God and the
Cosmologists* 1989(1), ch. 5 and in "Determinism and Reality" 1990(10)

[43] "Chance or Reality" 1981(3), p. 91.

[44] "Monkeys and Machine-Guns" 1986(12), p. 15. See also his quoting, in *The Savior of Science* 1988(1), p. 236, S. J. Gould's portrayal of G. G. Simpson as one "committed to the Darwinian view that variety is all and essence is an illusion."

[45] *The Road of Science and the Ways to God* 1978(2), p. 212.

[46] Ibid., p. 275.

[47] "The University and the Universe" 1982(1), p. 46.

[48] See "The Metaphysics of Discovery and the Rediscovery of Metaphysics" 1978(13), p. 194. In *The Relevance of Physics* 1966(1), p. 357, Jaki notes that "metaphysics, while being a step beyond science, is not a step beyond nature. Metaphysics is metascience but not metanature or a study independent of nature."

[49] Jaki discusses this discovery above all in *Cosmos and Creator* 1980(1), pp. 21-25, 36-44, and footnotes 31 (p. 144), 18 and 21 (p. 147), 24 (pp. 147-48), 26 (p. 148); in the Postscript to the new edition of *Science and Creation* 1986(1), pp. 361-69; *God and the Cosmologists* 1989(1), pp. 40-52. There is at least a brief discussion of the same in twenty of his other books or articles.

[50] This expression was used in *Time* (Oct. 30, 1978), p. 108; quoted in *Cosmos and Creator* 1980(1), pp. 21 and 37.

[51] "Religion and Science" 1981(6), p. 21.

[52] *The Savior of Science* 1988(1), p. 106.

[53] *Cosmos and Creator* 1980(1), p. 40.

[54] Ibid., p. 41.

[55] Chapter 4, "Anthropic Illusion," in *The Purpose of It All* 1990(1), is a full development of Jaki's views stated in "Order in Nature and Society" 1986(6), pp. 102-06; "From Scientific Cosmology to a Created Universe" 1982(4), pp. 256-59; and *God and the Cosmologists* 1989(1), pp. 189-190.

[56] *Cosmos and Creator* 1980(1), p. 41.

[57] Ibid.

[58] "The Absolute Beneath the Relative" 1985(3), pp. 32–35. In his Foreword to Pierre Duhem, *Medieval Cosmology* 1985(14), p. xiv, Jaki states: "As to relativity, the expansion of the universe and the 2.7°K cosmic background radiation stand out in bold defiance of the equivalence of all reference systems."

[59] Jaki insists on this in *The Road of Science and the Ways to God* 1978(2), p. 122; *The Savior of Science* 1988(1), p. 107; and *God and the Cosmologists* 1989(1), pp. 9–20.

[60] *The Paradox of Olbers' Paradox* 1969(2); "Das Gravitations-paradoxon des unendlichen Universums" 1979(1) and its English version in 1990(24).

[61] "The University and the Universe" 1982(1), pp. 52–53.

[62] *The Road of Science and the Ways to God* 1978(2), p. 269.

[63] "The Absolute Beneath the Relative" 1985(3), p. 35.

[64] See "God and Man's Science" 1984(4), p. 47, where Jaki states that "if the universe is not necessary, that is not necessarily what it is, then it is contingent. If, however, it is contingent, its actual shape and its very existence are dependent on a choice which transcends the entire universe. Such a choice or power can only be the creative omnipotence of God."

[65] Ibid., p. 44. In *Chesterton, A Seer of Science* 1986(4), pp. 96 and 153, Jaki notes that Popper, who uses the expression "all science is cosmology" (see K. R. Popper, *Conjectures and Refutations* [New York: Harper and Row, 1968] p. 136), did not invent this expression nor does he hold important consequences of it.

[66] "From Scientific Cosmology to a Created Universe" 1982(4), p. 260.

[67] See "God and Man's Science" 1984(4), pp. 47–48.

[68] "The History of Science and the Idea of an Oscillating Universe" 1984(9), pp. 159-160 and 165; Jaki notes that R. H. Dicke, in unpublished material, shows that the universe would be capable of about 1600 oscillations.

[69] Ibid., p. 158.

[70] "From Subjective Scientists to Objective Science" 1977(1), p. 328.

[71] *The Road of Science and the Ways to God* 1978(2), p. 257.

[72] *Cosmos and Creator* 1980(1), p. 54.

[73] "God and Man's Science" 1984(4), p. 49.

[74] "The Absolute beneath the Relative" 1985(3), p. 36. Jaki was the first to offer the extension of Gödel's theorem to cosmology in his *The Relevance of Physics* 1966(1), pp. 127-30. He further articulated it in *Cosmos and Creator* 1980(1), pp. 49-51, 54, 108; *The Savior of Science* 1988(1), pp. 108-09, 198; "From Scientific Cosmology to a Created Universe" 1982(4), pp. 257-58; *God and the Cosmologists* 1989(1), pp. 103-09.

[75] "The History of Science and the Idea of an Oscillating Universe" 1984(9), p. 164, footnote 50.

[76] For further details see "Miracles and Physics" 1987(5).

[77] "The History of Science and the Idea of an Oscillating Universe" 1984(9), p. 159.

[78] *The Road of Science and the Ways to God* 1978(2), p. 292.

Chapter Four

[1] *Chesterton, A Seer of Science* 1986(4), p.113.

[2] *Science and Creation* 1974(1), p. 139. See also *Cosmos and Creator* 1980(1), pp. 63-64, for the Near-Eastern world-picture.

[3] *Cosmos and Creator* 1980(1), p. 62.

[4] *The Savior of Science* 1988(1), p. 55. Here Jaki also states that the nondescriptness of the chaotic material "is so total as to be equivalent to complete darkness, which is probably the closest to which metaphorical language can go in suggesting non-being." See also "The Chaos of Scientific Cosmology" 1978(8), p. 103.

[5] *Cosmos and Creator* 1980(1), p. 62.

[6] Ibid., p. 63. In "The Universe in the Bible and in Modern Science" 1988(6), p. 138, Jaki notes that the word *bārā* does not "lend itself to a perfectly clear theological argument. The reason is its use at least three times in connection with human actions (Josh. 17:15, 18 and Ezek. 23:47)."

[7] *Science and Creation* 1974(1), pp. 147-148.

[8] "The Universe in the Bible and in Modern Science" 1988(6), p. 138.

[9] *Cosmos and Creator* 1980(1), p. 59.

[10] *Science and Creation* 1974(1), p. 147.

[11] Ibid., pp. 141-143 and see 2 Chron. 33:1-7, which Jaki quotes to recount Manasseh's 55-year-long reign encouraging idolatry.

[12] "Creation and Monastic Creativity"" 1985(12), p. 84. See Rom. 12:1.

[13] *Science and Creation* 1974(1), p. 158.

[14] See "The Greeks of Old and the Novelty of Science" 1983(5), pp. 276-277.

[15] *Cosmos and Creator* 1980(1), p. 67.

[16] *Science and Creation* 1974(1), p. 159.

[17] *Cosmos and Creator* 1980(1), p. 69.

[18] *Science and Creation* 1974(1), pp. 166-170.

[19] Origen, *On First Principles*, translation with Introduction and notes by G. W. Butterworth (London: Society for Promoting Christian Knowledge, 1936), pp. 87-88 (Book II, ch. iii); quoted by Jaki in *Science and Creation* 1974(1), p. 170.

[20] Origen, *Contra Celsum*, translation with Introduction and notes by H. Chadwick (Cambridge: University Press, 1953), p. 238; quoted by Jaki in *Science and Creation* 1974(1), p. 173.

[21] Saint Augustine, *De Civitate Dei*, Book XII, ch. 20, quoted by Jaki in *Science and Creation* 1974(1), p. 180.

[22] *Science and Creation* 1974(1), p. 183. Jaki refers to the English translation of Galileo's letter to the Grand Duchess Christina, in S. Drake, *Discoveries and Opinions of Galileo* (Garden City, New York: Doubleday, 1957) pp.173-216.

[23] *Science and Creation* 1974(1), p. 183.

[24] Ibid. Jaki refers to the edition by H. Vitelli of the Greek text of *Joannis Philoponi in Aristotelis physicorum libros quinque posteriores commentaria* (Berlin: G. Reimer, 1888), pp. 681-682 and 682-684 (Corollarium de inani), 639-642 (ad Lib. IV, cap. viii).

[25] *Planets and Planetarians* 1978(1), p. 39.

[26] *Cosmos and Creator* 1980(1), p. 70.

[27] "Creation and Monastic Creativity" 1985(12), p. 79.

[28] *Cosmos and Creator* 1980(1), pp. 71-72. See Tertullian, *De praescriptione haereticorum*, c. XIII, in PL 2:26.

[29] Fourth Lateran Council, Cap. 1, *De fide catholica*, "Definitio contra Albigenses et Cathares," in DS800. "We firmly believe . . . that there is only one true God . . . the Creator of all things, visible and invisible, who from the beginning of time made at once out of nothing both orders of creatures," in English translation in J. Neuner and J. Dupuis, *The Christian Faith in the Documents of the Catholic Church* (London: Collins, 1963), 19 (henceforth referred to as ND).

[30] *Cosmos and Creator* 1980(1), p. 75. Jaki refers to Saint Augustine, *De Civitate Dei*, Book XI, ch. 4-6, and Book XII, ch. 15-16 as the exposition of those arguments.

[31] "From Scientific Cosmology to a Created Universe" 1982(4), p. 259.

[32] "The Intelligent Christian's Guide to Scientific Cosmology" 1986(13), p. 125.

[33] *Cosmos and Creator* 1980(1) pp. 4, 54, 108 and p. 142 note 6. See also Saint Thomas Aquinas, *Summa Theologiae*, I, qu. 46, art. 2.

[34] "The Physics of Impetus and the Impetus of the Koran" 1985(7), p. 155.

[35] *Cosmos and Creator* 1980(1), pp. 84-85. See also First Vatican Council, *Dei Filius*, cap. 1, "De Deo rerum omnium creatore," in DS 3002 and cap. 2, "De revelatione," in DS 3004.

[36] "God and Creation" 1973(1), p. 112.

[37] *Cosmos and Creator* 1980(1), pp. 56 and 85. Jaki also remarks here that recent theological confusion could have its origin in a poorly developed notion of creation.

[38] *The Origin of Science and the Science of its Origin* 1978(5), p. 102.

[39] *The Savior of Science* 1988(1), pp. 21 and 34. See Vatican I, *Dei Filius*, cap. 2, "De revelatione," in DS 3005. "It is to be ascribed to this divine revelation that such truths among things divine which as of themselves are not beyond human reason can, even in the present condition of mankind, be known by everyone with facility, with firm certitude and with no admixture of error." English translation from ND 114.

[40] *The Savior of Science* 1988(1), p. 164. In *The Origin of Science and the Science of its Origin* 1978(5), p. 102, Jaki states that "the science of the future will loom threateningly ominous if man has to wear a blindfold about a sinful tragedy marking his origin."

[41] *Cosmos and Creator* 1980(1) p. 69.

⁴² Ibid., p. 76 and p. 153 note 30, where Jaki gives various interpretations of Philo's position.

⁴³ *The Origin of Science and the Science of its Origin* 1978(5), p. 71.

⁴⁴ *The Savior of Science* 1988(1), p. 72.

⁴⁵ "The Physics of Impetus and the Impetus of the Koran" 1985(7), p. 159. See also his review of Louis Bouyer, *Cosmos: Le monde et la gloire de Dieu* 1984(12), p. 306, where Jaki states that "Christology and creation are in fact two sides of the same coin which alone can really safeguard monotheism itself."

⁴⁶ *The Savior of Science* 1988(1), p. 73.

⁴⁷ "Creation and Monastic Creativity" 1985(12), p. 90.

⁴⁸ *The Savior of Science* 1988(1), pp. 76–77.

⁴⁹ *Cosmos and Creator* 1980(1), pp. 77–78.

Chapter Five

¹ *Chesterton, A Seer of Science* 1986(4), p. 80.

² *Cosmos and Creator* 1980(1), p. 41. The most comprehensive and recent work on this area is that of J. Barrow and F. Tipler, *The Anthropic Cosmological Principle* (Oxford: Clarendon Press, 1986), who thank Jaki in their preface (p. xii). Jaki states in a review, "Cosmic Stakes" 1986(11), p. 8, that this work "is indeed best in its technical aspects" and adds in *God and the Cosmologists* 1989(1), pp. 190-192, that Barrow and Tipler have repeatedly trapped themselves in wrong philosophical perspectives.

³ *Angels, Apes and Men* 1983(2), p. 81.

⁴ *The Road of Science and the Ways to God* 1978(2), p. 253, and also footnote 30, pp. 427-428, where it is noted that the origin of this expression is the Stoic phrase, *zoon logikon*, which Seneca renders as "rationale animal est homo" (*Epistulae morales ad Lucilium* 46:63). In

Christian usage, the phrase is deepened in meaning through belief in the immortality of the soul.

5 *The Road of Science and the Ways to God* 1978(2), p. 260.

6 *Angels, Apes and Men* 1983(2), pp. 75-76 and also p. 99, where Jaki states that "unlike an angel who needs no conquests, and unlike an ape uninterested in them, man thrives on conquests which are the fruit of a mysterious union in him of matter and mind."

7 Ibid,. p. 78.

8 Ibid., p. 99.

9 Ibid., p. 16.

10 Ibid. See also *The Road of Science and the Ways to God* 1978(2), p. 260, and footnote 65, p. 431. The expression was used by G. Ryle in *The Concept of Mind* (London: Hutchinson,1949), pp. 15-16; later it became the title of A. Koestler's book *The Ghost in the Machine* (New York: Macmillan, 1967). For Descartes' view of man, as discussed by Jaki, see also *The Relevance of Physics* 1966(1), pp. 285-286.

11 *Angels, Apes and Men* 1983(2), p. 20.

12 Ibid., p. 19.

13 Ibid., pp. 30-31 and 84. Jaki refers to Immanuel Kant, *Opus postumum*, ed. by A. Buchenau (Berlin: Walter de Gruyter, 1938), vol. 1, p. 145.

14 *Angels, Apes and Men* 1983(2), pp. 82-87.

15 Ibid., pp. 35-36, quoting G. W. F. Hegel, *Philosophy of Nature*, tr. M. J. Petry (London: George Allen and Unwin; New York: Humanities Press, 1969), vol. 3, pp. 2-3.

16 *The Road of Science and the Ways to God* 1978(2), p. 138.

17 *Angels, Apes and Men* 1983(2), p. 41. See ibid., p. 110, where Jaki quotes Maritain, who wrote: "Rousseau's man is Descartes' angel, playing

the beast"; J. Maritain, *Three Reformers: Luther—Descartes—Rousseau* (New York: Charles Scribner's Sons, 1929), p. 100.

[18] *Angels, Apes and Men* 1983(2), p. 48. See J. J. Rousseau, *Les rêveries d'un promeneur solitaire*, in *Oeuvres complètes de Jean Jacques Rousseau* (Paris: Bibliothèque de la Pléiade, 1964), vol. 1, p. 1046.

[19] *Angels, Apes and Men* 1983(2), p. 49. See *J. J. Rousseau, Emile*, translated by B. Foxley, with Introduction by A. B. de Monvel (London: J. M. Dent, 1974), p. 253.

[20] *Angels, Apes and Men* 1983(2), p. 50–55.

[21] Ibid., pp. 66–67.

[22] Ibid., p. 70.

[23] Ibid., p. 89 and note 65, p. 122, where Jaki notes how the "poetic flights of fancy of Teilhard de Chardin" have given the quoted phrase a "wide currency."

[24] *Cosmos and Creator* 1980(1), p. 115 and see note 9, p. 161.

[25] *The Relevance of Physics* 1966(1), pp. 283 and 315–16, where bionic batteries are discussed.

[26] *Chesterton, A Seer of Science* 1986(4), pp. 79–80.

[27] *Brain, Mind and Computers* 1969(1), p. 59.

[28] Ibid., p. 73.

[29] Ibid., pp. 53–54, where Jaki quotes D. R. Hartree, "The Eniac, an Electronic Computing Machine," in *Nature* 158 (1946), p. 505.

[30] "Brain, Mind and Computers" 1972(7), p. 15.

[31] *Brain, Mind and Computers* 1969(1), p. 137.

[32] "Brain, Mind and Computers" 1972(7), p. 16.

[33] *Brain, Mind and Computers* 1969(1), p. 146.

[34] "Brain, Mind and Computers" 1972(7), p. 16.

[35] *Brain, Mind and Computers* 1969(1), p. 195.

[36] Ibid., p. 168.

[37] See "Brain, Mind and Computers" 1972(7), p. 16.

[38] "Language, Logic, Logos" 1988(11), pp. 113, 125.

[39] *Brain, Mind and Computers* 1969(1), p. 224.

[40] "Language, Logic, Logos" 1988(11), p. 121.

[41] Ibid., pp. 111, 123.

[42] G. Pancaldi in *Scientia* 116 (1981), p. 158.

[43] That concept of the "plenitude" of God has been summed up by Jaki in *Cosmos and Creator* 1980(1), p. 127, as follows: "Since God's life is intellect, life and intellect must be everywhere in the universe." This necessitarian and a priori principle, heavily used in the eighteenth century, is not Christian in origin even though it was carelessly used by Christian thinkers.

[44] *Universal Natural History and Theory of the Heavens* 1981(1) pp. 182-196.

[45] *Cosmos and Creator* 1980(1), pp. 130. See also Chapter Two above, which dealt with the incompleteness in the progress of science.

[46] "Extraterrestrials and Scientific Progress" 1990(16). In "Religion and Science" 1981(6), p. 24, Jaki states: "One may suspect that the ridicule poured since Ockham on the question of universals may indeed turn out to be a boomerang. All advocates of ETI are in fact so many Ockhamist chickens come home to roost."

[47] *Cosmos and Creator* 1980(1), p. 118.

[48] Ibid., pp. 124-25.

[49] Ibid., p. 113.

[50] "Brain, Mind and Computers" 1972(7), p. 13.

[51] *Cosmos and Creator* 1980(1), p. 77.

[52] "Scientific Ethics and Ethical Science" 1974(2), p. 53; see also *The Origin of Science and the Science of its Origin* 1978(5), p. 106.

[53] *Cosmos and Creator* 1980(1), p. 114 and notes 5 and 6, p. 160.

[54] "Order in Nature and Society" 1986(6), pp. 100-101.

[55] "Scientific Ethics and Ethical Science" 1974(2), p. 49

[56] "Science: Revolutionary or Conservative?" 1989(4), p. 22.

[57] "Scientific Ethics and Ethical Science" 1974(2), p. 52.

[58] *The Relevance of Physics* 1966(1), p. 501, quoting P. R. Calder, "The Fragmentation of Science," in *The Advancement of Science* 12 (December 1955), p. 328.

[59] *The Relevance of Physics* 1966(1), p. 410, quoting the interview of Albert Einstein with Michael Amrine in *The New York Times Magazine*, June 23, 1946, p. 44.

[60] *The Road of Science and the Ways to God* 1978(2), p. 304; in note 46, p. 449, Jaki mentions that the statement was made in Boston on Nov. 10, 1948.

[61] "Scientific Ethics and Ethical Science" 1974(2), p. 52.

[62] See "Christ, Catholics and Abortion" 1985(4), pp. 7-15.

[63] "Ethics and the Science of Decision-Making in Business: A Specification of Perspectives" 1978(7), p. 151.

Chapter Six

[1] For a reference on Bolingbrooke's dictum, see *The Road of Science and the Ways to God* 1978(2), p. 328.

[2] See pp. 17-18, 20, and 38-39 above and *Uneasy Genius* 1984(1), pp. 421-36.

[3] A. N. Whitehead, *Science and the Modern World* (New York: The MacMillan Company, 1925) pp. 17-18. Jaki quotes in full the passage in question in *Science and Creation* 1974(1) pp. 230-31, and notes that Whitehead does not seem to have been familiar with Duhem at all. Most importantly, as Jaki notes in the same context, Whitehead, in line with his pantheism, does not refer to Christian belief in creation although it was the chief support of medieval scholastic rationality.

[4] *Science and Creation* 1974(1), p. 231.

[5] F. Copleston, *A History of Philosophy*, vol. 3, *Ockham to Suarez* (New York: Image Books, 1985), p. 158. Copleston attributes more to Ockham in the shaping of modern science than Jaki would. Copleston's conclusion (p. 167) is that "it is well to realize that the foundations of modern science were laid in medieval times. And it is well also to realize that the development of empirical science is in no way alien in principle to the Christian theology which formed the mental background in the Middle Ages. For if the world is the work of God it is obviously a legitimate and worth-while object of study."

[6] E. J. Dijksterhuis, *The Mechanization of the World Picture* (Oxford: University Press, 1961), Part, 2, sections 111-15.

[7] See A. C. Crombie, *Medieval and Early Modern Science* (Garden City, NY: Doubleday, 1959).

[8] See M. B. Foster, ""The Christian Doctrine of Creation and the Rise of Modern Science," in *Mind* 43 (1934), pp. 446-68; idem, "Christian Theology and Modern Science of Nature (I)," in *Mind* 44 (1935), pp. 439-66; idem, "Christian Theology and Modern Science of Nature (II)," in *Mind* 45 (1936), pp. 1-27.

[9] See L. Gilkey, *Maker of Heaven and Earth: The Christian Doctrine of Creation in the Light of Modern Knowledge* (Garden City, New York: Doubleday and Co., 1965), first published 1959. See also "The Role of Faith in Physics" 1967(2), p. 201.

[10] See G. B. Deason, "The Protestant Reformation and the Rise of Modern Science," in *Scottish Journal of Theology* 38 (1985), pp. 221-40; a list of authors of books and articles on this theme is found on p. 221 of his article.

[11] R. Hooykaas, *Religion and the Rise of Modern Science* (Edinburgh: Scottish Academic Press, 1972).

[12] D. M. MacKay, *Science, Chance and Providence* (Oxford: University Press, 1978), especially p. 11.

[13] E. Klaaren, *Religious Origins of Modern Science: Belief in Creation in Seventeenth-Century Thought* (Grand Rapids, Mich.: Eerdmans, 1977); and see Jaki's review of this work in *Theology Today* 35 (1979), pp. 496-97.

[14] V. Monod, *Dieu dans l'univers. Essai sur l'action exercée sur la pensée chrétienne par les grands systèmes cosmologiques depuis Aristôte jusqu'à nos jours* (Paris: Librairie Fischbacher, 1933).

[15] *Uneasy Genius* 1984(1), p. 421 note 173.

[16] C. A. Ronan, *The Cambridge Illustrated History of the World's Science* (Cambridge: University Press, 1983), pp. 266-68.

[17] Ibid., pp. 331-32.

[18] Ibid., p. 528. See T. S. Kuhn, *The Copernican Revolution* (Cambridge, Mass.: Harvard University Press, 1966), who traces the role of Philoponus, Buridan and Oresme in the rise of science but lays more importance on the Renaissance. In particular, Kuhn notes how the "turbulence of Europe during the Renaissance and Reformation itself facilitated Copernicus' astronomical innovation. . . . Radical innovations in science have repeatedly occurred during periods of national or international convulsion" (p. 123).

[19] Ronan, *The Cambridge Illustrated History of the World's Science*, pp. 186, 268 and 273.

[20] See F. R. Haig, Review of *The Road of Science and the Ways to God*, in Theological Studies 40 (1979), pp. 206–208.

21 For instance, M. Artigas, "Historia de la ciencia y teologia natural. Reflexiones en torno a la obra de Stanley L. Jaki," in *Scripta Theologica* (Pamplona) 13 (1981), p. 186, notes the vast and rigorously careful documentation of *The Road of Science and the Ways to God*.

[22] K. Cauthen, *Science, Secularization and God* (Nashville, Tenn.: Abingdon Press, 1969), p. 15–16.

[23] T. F. Torrance, *Divine and Contingent Order* (Oxford: University Press, 1981), p. 4 and p. 143 note 2.

[24] Ibid., p. 26: "nihil constat de contingentia nisi ex revelatione."

[25] L. Newbigin, *Foolishness to the Greeks. The Gospel and Western Culture* (London: SPCK, 1986), p. 70.

[26] P. E. Hodgson, "The Desecularization of Science," in W. Oddie (ed.), *After the Deluge* (London: SPCK, 1987), p. 118; also P. E. Hodgson, "A Duty to Share Knowledge," in *The Times* (April 27, 1985), p. 10.

[27] See L. Bouyer, *Cosmos et la gloire de Dieu* (Paris: Cerf, 1982), p. 34.

[28] K. J. Sharpe, "Stanley L. Jaki's Critique of Physics," in *Religious Studies* 18 (1982), p. 64.

[29] See *The Savior of Science* 1988(1), pp. 77 and 87.

[30] Sharpe, "Stanley L. Jaki's Critique of Physics," p. 75.

[31] A. R. Peacocke, Review of *Science and Creation*, in *Journal of Theological Studies* 16 (1975), p. 513.

[32] See D. C. Allison Jr., Review of *Cosmos and Creator*, in *The University Bookman* 26 (1986), p. 41.

[33] G. S. Hendry, "New Science, Old Apologetic" (Review of *The Road of Science and the Ways to God*), in *Theology Today* 36 (1979/1980), p. 262.

[34] *The Road of Science and the Ways to God* 1978(2), p. 35.

[35] Hendry, Review of *The Road of Science and the Ways to God,* p. 262.

[36] See *The Road of Science and the Ways to God* 1978(2), chapters 7-10 and 14-15, where Jaki lists and discusses the various philosophical pitfalls which were to plague science after its viable birth.

[37] Ibid., chapters 6, 11, and 12.

[38] Especially his letters from 1951 to his long-standing friend, M. Solovine. See *Cosmos and Creator* 1980(1), pp. 52-53.

[29] F. E. Budenholzer, Review of *The Road of Science and the Ways to God*, in *Zygon* 15 (1980), p. 248.

[40] See T. S. Torrance, Review of *Science and Creation*, in *Zygon* 11 (1976), p. 77.

[41] *Science and Creation* 1974(1), p. 53.

[42] K. F. Thibodeau, Review of *Science and Creation*, in *Isis* 67 (1976), p. 112.

[43] Jaki offered a sustained criticism of positivism for example in *The Relevance of Physics* 1966(1), chapter 11 and *The Road of Science and the Ways to God* 1978(2), chapter 10.

[44] W. J. Neidhardt, Review of *Science and Creation,* in *Journal of the American Scientific Affiliation* 27 (1975), p. 45.

[45] P. E. Hodgson, "The Significance of the Work of Stanley L. Jaki" in *The Downside Review* 105 (1987), p. 273.

[46] *The Paradox of Olbers' Paradox* 1969(2), ch. 10.

[47] *The Milky Way* 1972(1), ch. 8.

[48] "Das Gravitations-Paradoxon des unendlichen Universums" 1979(1) and its English version, 1990(24).

[49] *The Road of Science and the Ways to God* 1978(2), pp. 121–22.

[50] *God and the Cosmologists* 1989(1), pp. 9–12.

[51] Ibid., pp. 34–37.

[52] See ibid., and in Subject Index entries under "nothing(ness)."

[53] Ibid., pp. 41 and 43.

[54] Ibid., p. 53.

[55] P. Haffner, Review of *Chance or Reality* 1986(5), in *Gregorianum* 69 (1988), p. 598, an observation suggested by Fr. Willibrord Welten.

[56] *The Road of Science and the Ways to God* 1978(2), p. 274.

[57] *God and the Cosmologists* 1989(1), p. 208.

[58] Ibid., p. 53.

[59] See *The Savior of Science* 1988(1), pp. 233–34 and *God and the Cosmologists* 1989(1), p. 138.

[60] S. Weinberg, *The First Three Minutes: A Modern View of the Origin of the Universe* (London: André Deutsch, 1970), p. 7.

[61] J. D. Barrow and F. J. Tipler, *The Anthropic Cosmological Principle* (Oxford: Clarendon Press, 1986), p. 369.

[62] *God and the Cosmologists* 1989(1), pp. 157–63.

[63] Weinberg, *The First Three Minutes*, p. 138; also p. 139, where Weinberg raises the possibility of an "absolute zero" of time, "beyond which it is in principle impossible to trace any chain of cause and effect."

[64] *God and the Cosmologists* 1989(1), p. 81. Hodgson echoes this when he states: "It is not possible to show scientifically of any state that there can

be no antecedent state." See Hodgson, "The Desecularization of Science," p. 137.

[65] Hodgson, "The Desecularization of Science," p. 142.

[66] *Cosmos and Creator* 1980(1), p. 102. St. Thomas Aquinas, *Summa theologiae*, I, qu. 16, art. 1: "esse rei, non veritas eius, causat veritatem intellectus" ("the being of the thing, not its truth, is the cause of truth in the intellect"). See also p. 42 above.

[67] *Cosmos and Creator* 1980(1), p. 103.

[68] "Evicting the Creator" 1988(9) and *God and the Cosmologists* 1989(1), pp. 90–95.

[69] "Determinism and Reality" 1990(10). In his *A Brief History of Time* (London: Bantam Press, 1988), p. 55, S. W. Hawking states that "Heisenberg's uncertainty principle is a fundamental, inescapable property of the world," without realizing the anti-ontological consequences of this meaning, first attached, as Jaki showed, by Heisenberg himself to that principle. The same point is wholly overlooked by J. Polkinghorne in his review of *God and the Cosmologists* in *Theology,* 63 (1990), p. 407. There he claims that Jaki rejects quantum mechanics, which Jaki never did. Jaki, who from his *Relevance of Physics* 1966(1) on has spoken with the greatest admiration for quantum mechanics, never failed to distinguish it from the Copenhagen antiontology grafted on it by Heisenberg and Bohr. Failure to see this crucial distinction is what defeats R. J. Russell's defense of Bohr against Jaki's "vitriolic" anti-Bohr remarks. See R. J. Russell, "Quantum Physics in Philosophical and Theological Perspective," in R. J. Russell, W. R. Stoeger, and G. V. Coyne (eds.), *Physics, Philosophy, and Theology: A Common Quest for Understanding* (Vatican City State: Vatican Observatory, 1988), p. 372 note 20. At any rate, Russell uses the term "vitriolic" in disregard of its standard definition.

[70] Hawking, *A Brief History of Time*, pp. 136-37.

[71] *God and the Cosmologists* 1989(1), p. 106. See also "Evicting the Creator" 1988(9), p. 20.

[72] Hawking, *A Brief History of Time*, pp. 136 and 141.

[73] Jaki's concern for the centrality of the universe in scientific as well as philosphical discourse is the theme of the book, *Is There a Universe?*, he is now writing. There he probes into the baffling indifference of modern scientific cosmologists to demonstrate first the existence of the universe before dealing with it scientifically. The book includes an analysis of various claims according to which the existence of the universe is indemonstrable and comes to a close with a positive answer, in the form of a new demonstration, to the question posed in the title.

Chapter Seven

[1] F. Copleston, *A History of Philosophy*, vol. 2, *Augustine to Scotus* (New York: Image Books, 1985), p. 140.

[2] See ch. 3 in *The Road of Science and the Ways to God* 1978(2)

[3] E. Gilson, *The Unity of Philosophical Experience* (1937; Westminster, Md.: Christian Classics, 1982), p. 66.

[4] *The Road of Science and the Ways to God* 1978(2), pp. 40–41 where he also notes that Ockham could not accept the notion of universally valid scientific laws as expressive of causal interaction among material entities.

[5] Particularly revealing in this respect is Jaki's remark that according to Ockham it was possible to speak of starlight without assuming the existence of stars (ibid., p. 42).

[6] *The Road of Science and the Ways to God* 1978(2), p. 43.

[7] Ibid., ch. 6.

[8] Ibid., chs. 4 and 5.

[9] *The Relevance of Physics* 1966(1), pp. 468–85. See also *The Road of Science and the Ways to God* 1978(2), pp. 148–49.

[10] *The Road of Science and the Ways to God* 1978(2), pp. 150–51.

[11] Carnap urged the avoidance of even such "abstract" terms as wire and copper, and their replacement with circumlocutions such as "long thin brown body." See ibid., p. 221. Jaki finds the most telling example of Reichenbach's inability to cope with reality in his admission that one cannot be absolutely certain even of one's own existence. See *God and the Cosmologists*, p. 224.

[12] *The Road of Science and the Ways to God* 1978(2), p. 228.

[13] Ibid., pp. 155-56.

[14] See *Uneasy Genius* 1984(1), pp. 320 and 325. Duhem also manifests in his art that perception of reality which is congruent with his essentially realist position; see *The Physicist as Artist* 1988(3).

[15] *Prémices philosophiques* 1987(3).

[16] *The Road of Science and the Ways to God* 1978(2), ch. 15 and "Science: Revolutionary or Conservative?" 1989(4).

[17] See "The Metaphysics of Discovery and the Rediscovery of Metaphysics" 1978(13). With his argumentation Jaki clearly preceded D. Antiseri, "Il ruolo della Metafisica nella scoperta scientifica e nella storia della scienza" in *Rivista di Filosofia Neo-Scolastica* 74 (1982), pp. 68-108.

[18] See *The Relevance of Physics* 1966(1), p. 505.

[19] Ibid., ch. 15 and especially pp. 235-37. Here again Jaki was ahead of a similar argument made by R. J. Blackwell, "A New Direction in the Philosophy of Science," in *The Modern Schoolman* 59 (1981- 1982), pp. 55-59. In the light of that ch. 15, the article by R. N. Giere, "Philosophy of Science Naturalized," in *Philosophy of Science* 52 (1985), pp. 331-56, should appear as an approval of the effort to do such philosophy in disregard of metaphysics.

[20] *Brain, Mind and Computers* 1969(1), p. 207.

[21] "Language, Logic, Logos" 1988(11).

[22] Ibid., pp. 95-99.

[23] *God and the Cosmologists* 1989(1), pp. 96-97.

[24] *The Relevance of Physics* 1966(1), pp. 343–45; *The Road of Science and the Ways to God* 1978(2), p. 257; *God and the Cosmologists* 1989(1), pp. 95–96.

[25] *The Road of Science and the Ways to God* 1978(2), p. 213.

[26] "Determinism and Reality" 1990(10).

[27] *The Relevance of Physics* 1966(1), pp. 385–88; *The Purpose of It All* 1990(1), pp. 184–85.

[28] *Miracles and Physics* 1989(2), see especially the introduction where Jaki speaks of the acceptance of miracles as a crucial test of one's epistemological realism.

[29] A variant on the title, "The Horns of Complementarity," of ch. 13 of *The Road of Science and the Ways to God* 1978(2).

[30] See ibid., pp. 212–13.

[31] *The Purpose of It All* 1990(1), pp. 121–23, 137–41.

[32] Ibid. pp. 132–37.

[33] Ibid., pp. 141–44.

[34] Jaki's first use of the term "Aquikantism" is in *The Keys of the Kingdom* 1986(3) p. 157. See also *The Savior of Science* 1988(1), pp. 115, 212 and 252.

[35] It was at Jaki's urging that P. Trower translated into English Gilson's *Le réalisme méthodique* (1935); see 1990(29).

[36] *The Purpose of It All* 1990(1). p. 169. Here Jaki follows the reasonings which Gilson set forth in his *From Aristotle to Darwin and Back Again* (Notre Dame, IN: University of Notre Dame Press, 1984), translated, at Jaki's urging, by J. Lyon. For an earlier discussion by Jaki of the philosophy of being, see *The Keys of the Kingdom* 1986(3), pp. 158–60.

[37] F. E. Budenholzer, Review of *The Road of Science and the Ways to God*, *Zygon* 15 (1980), pp. 248–49.

[38] Unpublished paper read at a Conference, held at Maynouth College (Ireland) in 1973, on Lonergan's freshly published *Method*.

[39] This statement of Newman from the Introduction to the *Essay on the Development of Christian Doctrine* is used by Jaki in his introduction to the collection of essays, *Newman Today*, edited by him. See 1989(9), pp. 10-11.

[40] "The Theological Aspects of Creative Science" 1976(2), pp. 154 and 160.

[41] This was true even of Einstein, who made some disparaging remarks about some priests who tried to show the theistic perspective behind his cosmology. See *Cosmos and Creator* 1980(1), pp. 52-53.

[42] *The Savior of Science* 1988(1), pp. 33-34.

[43] *Cosmos and Creator* 1980(1), pp. 98-102.

[44] *God and the Cosmologists* 1989(1), pp. 84, 94 and 104. As has been remarked (see p. 160, note 73), Jaki is now working out a philosophical way, independent of scientific astronomy and cosmology, of knowing that there is a strict totality of things. He gave a first glimpse of his ideas at a seminar he was invited to give in the Department of Astronomy of the University of Arizona (Phoenix), on February 18, 1991. A more formal presentation was the paper he had been invited to deliver at the Pontifical Academy in Cracow on May 9, 1991.

[45] Ibid., pp. 235-36.

[46] Ibid., pp. 214-21. There he listed not only humanists but also scientists!

[47] This insistence by Jaki on science, as a method dealing with things in motion, is relatively new in his writings. See *The Savior of Science* 1988(1), pp. 46-47. Since then he made heavy reliance on it in his "Universe and Science" and "Beyond Science," papers delivered in Spain and California, respectively, both to be published soon.

[48] Jaki first called attention to pantheism as widespread among Jewish intellectuals in *Cosmos and Creator* 1980(1), p. 153, note 31.

[49] The same book contains Jaki's first discussion (p. 71) of the cosmological significance of the christological expression, "only begotten." For further elaboration, see *The Savior of Science* 1988(1), pp. 72-75.

[50] "The Holy Roman Church most firmly believes, professes and preaches that the one true God, Father, Son and Holy Spirit, is the Creator of all things visible and invisible, who *when He so willed*, out of His bounty made all creatures, spiritual as well as corporeal" DS 1733 (italics added). English translation from ND 408. The importance of the italicized words was noted by C. Tresmontant, *Christian Metaphysics* (Dublin: Gill and Son, 1965), p. 53.

[51] Vatican I. See DS 3002 and 3025.

[52] "Language, Logic, Logos" 1988(11), p. 126.

[53] *Cosmos and Creator* 1980(1), p. 80.

[54] Hawking, *A Brief History of Time*, pp. 173-74.

[55] "Evicting the Creator" 1988(9).

[56] What Jaki had already noted in *Science and Creation* 1974(1) (see pp. 70-71) about the inconsistencies of Egyptian calendar making, he pointedly recalled in his Templeton Prize Address 1987(4) in reference to the Council of Trent's decision about the calendar reform. His particular target was a remark of Winston Churchill who equated pagan Egyptian priests with Catholic priests sitting at the Council of Trent and tried to create the impression that nothing had really changed in the previous two thousand years.

[57] *The Savior of Science* 1988(1), pp. 81-82.

[58] M. Schmaus, *God and Creation — Dogma 2* (Kansas City: Sheed and Ward, 1969), p. 77.

[59] "Language, Logic, Logos" 1988(11), p. 126. See also *The Savior of Science* 1988(1), pp. 76-77, and 79. Jaki is certainly original in calling attention to the fact that in upholding against Arius the strict divinity of the Logos, Athanasius also stressed the full rationality of the cosmos as a necessary consequence of its having been created by such a Logos.

[60] See Vatican I in DS 3004.

[61] Jaki spoke to me repeatedly about one such case, involving a very prominent Reformed theologian, still living.

[62] See *The Savior of Science* 1988(1), p. 199, and *The Purpose of It All* 1990(1), p. 144, where he refers to H. de Lubac's defense of Teilhard's personal orthodoxy.

[63] *The Purpose of It All* 1990(1), pp. 141–44.

[64] J. A. Lyons, *The Cosmic Christ in Origen and Teilhard de Chardin* (New York: Oxford University Press, 1982), p. 153. Jaki finds very inadequate Teilhard's idea of the cosmic initial point (Alpha) as well as his distinction between matter and mind. See *Cosmos and Creator* 1980(1), p. 15.

[65] See Vatican II, Dogmatic Constitution *Lumen gentium*, 16.

[66] See ch. 12 in *Science and Creation* 1974(1) and "The Modernity of the Middle Ages" 1987(13), and "Medieval Christianity: Its Inventiveness in Technology and Science" (forthcoming). See also E. L. Mascall, *Christian Theology and Natural Science* (London: Longmans, 1956), pp. 97–98.

[67] Vatican II, Declaration *Nostra aetate* on the Relation of the Church to non-Christian Religions, 2.2.

[68] Vatican II, Decree *Ad gentes divinitus*, on the Church's Missionary Activity, 8, 9.2

[69] See ch. 8 "The Cultivation of Purpose," in *The Purpose of It All* 1990(1).

[70] This charge was first made in a conspicuous form by L. White Jr. in the full glare of the annual meeting of the American Association for the Advancement of Science and published as "The Historical Roots of our Ecological Crisis," *Science* 155 (1967), pp. 1203–07. Jaki first took issue with White's claim in *The Road of Science and the Ways to God* 1978(1), p. 450.

[71] "The Three Faces of Technology" 1988(7).

[72] "Ecology or Ecologism," an invited essay, which Jaki read at the joint meeting of the Pontifical Academy of Sciences and of the Swedish Royal Academy of Sciences, on the ecological role of rain forests, held in the Vatican in May 1990, to be published in the Proceedings of that meeting.

[73] He did so by quoting, repeatedly, a letter, published in the *New York Times,* by the historian of science, Pearce L. Williams, who argued that since in a purely consensual society no one can appeal to a "higher morality" and that since moral consensus is rapidly weakening in modern society, the latter is on its road to anarchy. See *The Only Chaos and Other Essays* 1990(2), pp. 42 and 100.

[74] "Normalcy as Terror: The Naturalization of AIDS" 1987(14).

[75] See ch. 19, "The Ethos of Science," in *The Road of Science and the Ways to God* 1978(1).

[76] G. K. Chesterton, *Orthodoxy* (New York: Image Books, 1959), p. 15. See *Chesterton, A Seer of Science* 1986(4), pp. 184-86.

[77] The last phrase in *The Relevance of Physics* 1966(1), p. 533.

[78] "Every man's work, whether it be literature or music or pictures or architecture or anything else, is always a portrait of himself." S. Butler, *The Way of All Flesh* (New York: The New American Library, 1960), p. 60.

[79] *Scientist and Catholic: Pierre Duhem* 1991(1) and its French translation, *Pierre Duhem: Homme de foi et de science* 1991(2)

[80] He plans to present the evidence in an essay with the title, "The Duhem Scandal."

Chapter Eight

[1] Second Vatican Council, *Lumen Gentium* 1.

[2] K. J. Sharpe, "Stanley L. Jaki's Critique of Physics," *Religious Studies* 18 (1982), p. 73.

[3] *The Savior of Science* 1988(1), pp. 33-34, and 184-86.

[4] C. Longley, in *The Times* (London), May 12, 1987.

[5] Following his public lectures, Jaki has often been challenged for a debate by six-day creationists.

[6] Such grounds are the metaphysical principles of continuity in nature, the honor due to secondary causation, and especially the mind's ability to postulate connections where they are not supplied by empirical data. See *The Savior of Science*, pp. 136-38.

[7] Such a group is represented by *The Asbury Theological Journal*, connected with Asbury Theological Seminary, in Wilmore Kentucky.

[8] A case in point is the effort of the editor of the *Journal of the American Scientific Affiliation*, who, in order to undercut Jaki's defense of mind-body dualism in "Brain, Mind, and Computers" 1972(7), interrupted its text in the same issue with an insert which, by implication, denied the immortality of the soul.

[9] *And on This Rock* 1978(4) and 1987(1), *The Keys of the Kingdom* 1986(3).

[10] "G. K. C. as R. C." 1986(18).

[11] A favorite phrase of C. S. Lewis and the title of his book, first published in 1952.

[12] *The Savior of Science* 1988(1), pp. 196 and 249.

[13] R. V. Young, "Faith and Science in a Contingent Universe" (Review of *The Road of Science and the Ways to God*) in *Faith and Reason* 6 (1980), p. 81. Hodgson (another Catholic) further elaborates on Jaki's contribution to the life of the Church as follows: "In this age of science when the study of the history of science is supplanting the study of classical literature as the formative matrix of human values, he, more than any other Catholic writer, provides safe perspectives and vast documentation for a truly Catholic view of science. The perspective is Catholic and universal because it includes the great theological facts of history, the very facts that the secularist historiographers of science try to ignore or minimize. . . . He has set his face against the forces that are undermining

the Church, and in so doing has articulated the anguish of the People of God." See Hodgson, "The Significance of the Work of Stanley L. Jaki," pp. 272 and 273.

[14] The organization in question has its center in Ann Arbor, Michigan. Personal communication from Jaki.

[15] *Scienza e Non Credenza* (Città del Vaticano: Segretariato per i Non Credenti, 1980), p. 225. English version from *Atheism and Dialogue* 14 (1979), p. 112.

[16] F. Ferré, Review of *The Road of Science and the Ways to God* in *Journal of Religion* 60 (1980), p. 89, where he finds Jaki's tone polemical and adds (p. 90) that he wished Jaki gave evidence of "listening with a little more openness of mind and speaking with a little more generosity of spirit." Jaki, of course, could rightly ask whether Ferré and others are listening with any openness of mind to the vast evidence and concise arguments presented by him.

[17] M. Artigas, "Historia de la ciencia y teología natural. Reflexiones en torno a la obra de Stanley L. Jaki," *Scripta Theologica* (Pamplona) 13 (1981), pp. 200-201. Jaki's influence on Artigas' thought may also be seen in Artigas' essays, "Física y creación: el origen del universo" in *Scripta Theologica* (Pamplona) 19 (1987), pp. 347-73 and "La obra di Stanley L. Jaki" in *Ciencia, Fe, Cultura* 1990(8), pp. 5-21.

[18] Herbert Feigl, unpublished letter to S. L. Jaki, Jan. 9, 1969.

[19] Karl Popper, unpublished letter to S. L. Jaki, April 5, 1982.

[20] F. Russo, "The Evangelization and Pastoral Care of Scientists and Technologists," in *Apostolate of Culture, The Laity Today* 28 (1981), p. 96.

[21] "Science for Catholics" 1986(16), pp. 7-8.

[22] Russo, "The Evangelization and Pastoral Care of Scientists and Technologists," p. 99.

[23] Ibid., p. 109.

[24] See Congregation for the Doctrine of Faith, *Instruction on the Ecclesial Vocation of the Theologian* (Vatican City: Libreria Editrice Vaticana, 1990).

[25] Second Vatican Council, *Lumen Gentium* 23.1

[26] J. H. Newman, *An Essay on the Development of Christian Doctrine* (new ed.; London: Basil Montagu Pickering, 1878), p. 7.

[27] See *Les tendences nouvelles de l'ecclésiologie* 1957(1); *And on This Rock* 1978(4) and 1987(1); *The Keys of the Kingdom* 1986(3).

[28] *The Discourses of the Popes from Pius XI to John Paul II to the Pontifical Academy of Sciences 1936-1986* (Vatican City: Pontifical Academy of Sciences, 1986), pp. 73-84 (to be referred to as *Discourses of the Popes*). Jaki discusses this address of Pius XII in *The Relevance of Physics* 1966(1), pp. 448-50; *Science and Creation* 1974(1), p. 347; *Cosmos and Creator* 1980(1), pp. 18-20.

[29] *Discourses of the Popes*, p. 82.

[30] E. T. Whittaker, *Space and Spirit: Theories of the Universe and the Arguments for the Existence of God* (London: Thomas Nelson, 1946), p. 118. See *Discourses of the Popes*, p. 83.

[31] *The Relevance of Physics* 1966(1), p. 449. *Cosmos and Creator* 1980(1), p. 18.

[32] Ibid.

[33] *Discourses of the Popes*, p. 82.

[34] Hawking, *A Brief History of Time* (London: Bantam Press, 1988), pp. 46-47.

[35] "Evicting the Creator" 1988(9), p. 20.

[36] Jaki notes in *The Relevance of Physics* 1966(1), p. 450, that a year later in his address to the International Meeting of Astronomers the Pope advised great caution. Indeed, the Pope declared: "There is still a long way to go, and it seems that the quest will be endless. It is quite unlikely that even the most gifted enquirer will succeed in recognising (and much

less solving) all the mysteries locked up in the cosmos." Quoted from P. J. McLaughlin, *The Church and Modern Science* (New York: Philosophical Library, 1957), p. 192. It was in that discourse that the Pope characterized as "gratuitous" the continuous, ongoing "creation" of hydrogen atoms, claimed by steady-state theorists. Jaki has been practically alone among Catholic philosophers and historians of science in his criticism of this basic claim of steady-state theorists which strikes at the very heart of Christian dogma. Furthermore, he did not refrain from referring to the Pope's criticism of that theory. See *Cosmos and Creator* 1980(1), p. 20.

[37] Second Vatican Council, *Gaudium et Spes* 36.

[38] *The Savior of Science* 1988(1), p. 68.

[39] For Jaki's criticism of scientism, see pp. 22-24 above.

[40] April 23, 1966, in *Discourses of the Popes*, p. 120.

[41] April 27, 1968, in *Discourses of the Popes*, p. 127.

[42] *Credo of the People of God* (1968; London: Catholic Truth Society, 1971), p. 4.

[43] Pope Paul VI, in connection with the Apollo 10 Moon-landing in *Insegnamenti di Paolo VI* (Vatican City: Vatican Polyglot Press, 1963-1978), 7 (1969), pp. 491-92 (to be referred to as *IP*).

[44] *Cosmos and Creator* 1980(1), p. 141.

[45] *IP* 15 (1977), pp. 141-43.

[46] *L'Osservatore Romano* (Weekly English Edition), Nov. 24, 1980, p. 7 (to be referred to as *ORE*).

[47] *Discourses of the Popes*, p. 170.

[48] See pp. 24-29 above.

[49] *L'Osservatore Romano* (Daily Italian Edition), July 15, 1985, p. 1 (to be referred to as *OR*).

[50] *Discourses of the Popes*, p. 162.

[51] See pp. 42, 45, 48, 82, 90-91, 105 above.

[52] *Insegnamenti di Giovanni Paolo II* (Vatican City: Vatican Polyglot Press, 1978 -), 3 (1980), p. 1784 (to be referred to as *IG*).

[53] *ORE* March 17, 1986, p. 1.

[54] *OR* Sept. 27, 1987, p. 4.

[55] Discourse at the Fiftieth Anniversary of the Pontifical Academy of Sciences (Oct. 28, 1986), in *Discourses of the Popes*, p. 197.

[56] *ORE* Nov. 24, 1980, p. 6.

[57] *Discourses of the Popes*, p. 162.

[58] *ORE* Jan. 13, 1986, p. 2.

[59] *ORE* Jan. 20, 1986, p. 5.

[60] Letter to the Director of the Vatican Observatory (June 1, 1988) in *OR* Oct. 26, 1988, p. 6.

[61] A series of eight lectures to be given by Jaki on "Genesis 1 through History" is scheduled for March 25-28, 1992, at the University of Notre Dame.

[62] *ORE* Febr. 3, 1986, p. 8.

[63] *ORE* Jan. 20, 1986, p. 5.

[64] *ORE* Feb. 3, 1986, p. 8. For Jaki's line of argument see pp. 59-63 and 109 above.

[65] *ORE* Apr. 14, 1986, p. 11. Cardinal Ratzinger has also stressed that "It is not accidental that the Apostles' Creed begins with the confession: 'I believe in God, the Father Almighty, Creator of heaven and earth.' This primordial faith in the Creator God (a God who is really God) forms the pivot, as it were, about which all the other Christian truths turn. If

vacillation sets in here, all the rest comes tumbling down." J. Card.
Ratzinger and V. Messori, *The Ratzinger Report* (Leominster, England:
Fowler Wright Books, 1985), p. 78.

[66] *OR* Apr. 13, 1986, p. 5.

Publications of Stanley L. Jaki

1951

1. "Protestáns visszhang — Katolikus válasz" ["Protestant Echo — Catholic Reply"], *Katolikus Szemle* ["Catholic Review," published in Rome in Hungarian], 3 (1951), pp. 32-34 in 4°.

1952

1. "Uj törekvések as Egyház hivö megértésére" ["New Trends toward a Spiritual Understanding of the Church"], *Katolikus Szemle* 4 (1952), pp. 19-22 in 4°.

1953

1. "Stockholmtól Lundig: Az ekuménikus mozgalom iránya és szelleme" ["From Stockholm to Lund: The Direction and Spirit of the Ecumenical Movement"], *Katolikus Szemle* 5 (1953), pp. 16-19 in 4°.

1954

1. "Ekuménikus Kongresszus Evanstonban" ["Ecumenical Congress in Evanston"], *Katolikus Szemle* 6 (1954), pp. 103-107 in 4°.

2. "Szent Pál — Krisztus harsonája" ["Saint Paul: Christ's Trumpet"], *A Délamerikai Magyar Hirlap Evkönyve* ["Yearbook of the South-American Hungarian News"], Sao Paolo: Délamerikai Magyar Hirlap, 1954, pp. 19-23.

3. "In His Image," *Image* [mimeographed Literary Bulletin of Saint Vincent Seminary, Latrobe, Pa.] 1/2 (May 1954), pp. 3-6.

4. "Istenhez láncolva" ["Chained to God"], *Délamerikai Magyar Hirlap*, March 21, 1954.

5. "Krisztus mint regényhös" ["Christ as novel-hero"], *Délamerikai Magyar Hirlap*, March 28, April 4, and April 11, 1954.

6. "Három R és ami utána következik" ["The Three R's and Beyond"], *Délamerikai Magyar Hirlap*, April 25, 1954.

7. "Az éhes emberiség" ["Mankind in the Grip of Hunger"], *Délamerikai Magyar Hirlap*, May 2, 1954.

8. "Kereszténység és irodalom" ["Christianity and Literature"], *Délamerikai Magyar Hirlap*, May 9, and May 16, 1954).

9. "Ismét a három R" ["The Three R's Again"], Délamerikai Magyar Hirlap, May 23, 1954).

10. "Washington magyar ezredese" ["Washington's Hungarian Colonel"], *Délamerikai Magyar Hirlap* , June 6, 1954.

11. "Magyar fiataloknak: Gettysburgtól a Don Kanyarig" ["To Young Hungarians: From Gettysburg to the Don's Bend"], *Délamerikai Magyar Hirlap,* June 13, 1954.

12. "McCarthy és a macartizmus" ["McCarthy and McCarthyism"], *Délamerikai Magyar Hirlap*, July 4, 1954.

13. "Az én rögeszmém" ["My Fixed Idea"], *Délamerikai Magyar Hirlap*, July 4, 1954.

1956

1. "Chance and Evolution," *Civitas Dei: A Magyar Katolikus Tudományos és Müvészeti Akadémia Káldi György Társasága Évkönyve* ["Yearbook of the Káldi György Society of the Hungarian Catholic Academy of Arts and Sciences"] (Saint Norbert College, West De Père, Wis.: 1956), pp. 46-67.

1957

1. *Les tendances nouvelles de l'ecclésiologie* [Doctoral Dissertation for S.T.D., Pontificio Ateneo S. Anselmo, Roma, 1950] (Rome: Herder and Herder, 1957), 274pp.

1958

1. "A Study of the Distribution of Radon, Thoron, and Their Decay Products above and below the Ground," jointly with Victor F. Hess, *Journal of Geophysical Research* 63 (1958), pp. 373-390.

2. "A csillagászat új utjai" ["The New Paths of Astronomy"], *Katolikus Szemle* 10 (1958), pp. 26-32.

3. "A világegyetem kialakulása" ["The Evolution of the Universe"], *Katolikus Szemle* 10 (1958), pp. 71-78.

4. "Az élet eredete" ["The Origin of Life"], *Katolikus Szemle* 10 (1958), pp. 123-129.

5. "Van-e élet más égitesteken?" ["Is There Life on Other Celestial Bodies?"], *Katolikus Szemle* 10 (1958), pp. 169-176.

1959

1. "The Ecclesiology of Abbot Vonier," *The American Benedictine Review* 10 (1959), pp. 163-175.

2. "Relativitás és abszolutum" ["Relativity and the Absolute"], *Katolikus Szemle* 11 (1959), pp. 41-54.

3. "A világür küszöbén: A Nemzetközi Geofizikai év eredményei" ["On the Threshold of Outer Space: The Results of the International Geophysical Year"], *Katolikus Szemle* 11 (1959), pp. 123-134.

4. "Hit és tudomány Newton müveiben" ["Faith and Science in Newton's Works"], *Katolikus Szemle* 11 (1959), pp. 210-220.

1960

1. "A titokzatos anyag" ["The Mysterious Matter"], *Katolikus Szemle* 12 (1960), pp. 132-136 and 203-211.

1961

1. "A klasszikus fizika utja" ("The Road of Classical Physics"), *Katolikus Szemle* 13 (1961), pp. 42-53

2. "A titókzatos gravitáció," ["The Mysterious Gravitation"], *Katolikus Szemle* 13 (1961), pp. 125-136.

3. "Rádiocsillagászat" ["Radioastronomy"], *Katolikus Szemle* 13 (1961), pp. 210-219.

4. "A természettudomány születése" ["The Birth of Natural Science"], *Katolikus Szemle* 13 (1961), pp. 282-293.

1962

1. "A modern tudomány kezdetei" ["The Beginnings of Modern Science"], *Katolikus Szemle* 14 (1962), pp. 134-144.

1963

1. *Les tendances nouvelles de l'ecclésiologie*, reprinting of 1957(1).

1965

1. "Uj fejezet a csillagászatban?" ["A New Chapter in Astronomy?"], *Katolikus Szemle* 17 (1965), pp. 77-79.

2. "Van-e élet más égitesteken?" ["Is There Life on Other Celestial Bodies?"], *Katolikus Szemle* 17 (1965), pp. 362-365.

1966

1. *The Relevance of Physics* (Chicago: University of Chicago Press, 1966), 640pp.

1967

1. "Recent Orthodox Ecclesiology," English translation by J. M. Desjardins of pp. 99-105 of 1957(1), *Diakonia* 2 (1967), pp. 250-265.

2. "The Role of Faith in Physics," *Zygon* 2 (1967), pp. 187-202.

3. "Olbers', Halley's, or Whose Paradox?" *American Journal of Physics* 35 (1967), pp. 200-210.

1969

1. *Brain, Mind and Computers* (New York: Herder and Herder, 1969), 267pp.

2. *The Paradox of Olbers' Paradox: A Case History of Scientific Thought* (New York: Herder and Herder, 1969), 269pp.

3. "Goethe and the Physicists," *American Journal of Physics* 37 (1969), pp. 195-203.

4. Introductory Essay to *Pierre Duhem. To Save the Phenomena: An Essay on the Idea of Physical Theory from Plato to Galileo*, trans. E. Doland and C. Maschler (Chicago: University of Chicago Press, 1969), pp. ix-xxvi.

1970

1. *Festrede am Jubiläumstage der Olbers-Gesellschaft* (Bremen: [Olbers Gesellschaft], 1970), 15pp.

2. "Olbers als Kosmologe," *Nachrichten der Olbers Gesellschaft* 79 (October 1970), pp. 5-13 in 4°.

3. "Drei kosmologische Vorträge von Wilhelm Olbers," *Nachrichten der Olbers Gesellschaft* 79 (October 1970), pp. 14-28.

4. "New Light on Olbers' Dependence on Chéseaux," *Journal for the History of Astronomy* 1 (1970), pp. 53-55.

5. "Re: 'Jaki and Goethe'," *American Journal of Physics* 38 (1970), p. 546.

6. *The Relevance of Physics*, reprint of 1966(1).

1971

1. "The Milky Way before Galileo," *Journal for the History of Astronomy* 2 (1971), pp. 161-167.

2. "Le Prix Lecomte du Nouy: Discours de remerciements. Rev. Stanley Jaki, Lauréat du Prix américain Lecomte du Nouy," *Cahiers de l'Association Lecomte du Nouy* 3 (Spring 1971), pp. 9-15.

1972

1. *The Milky Way: An Elusive Road for Science* (New York: Science History Publications; Newton Abbott, England: David & Charles, 1972), xi + 352 pp.

2. Address given on accepting the Lecomte du Nouy Prize for 1970, *Cahier bilingue de l'Association Lecomte du Nouy* (Spring 1972), pp. 48-54.

3. "The Original Formulation of the Titius-Bode Law," *Journal for the History of Astronomy* 3 (1972), pp. 136-138.

4. "The Milky Way from Galileo to Wright," *Journal for the History of Astronomy* 3 (1972), pp. 199-204.

5. "Das Titius-Bodesche Gesetz im Licht der Originaltexte," *Nachrichten der Olbers Gesellschaft* 86 (October 1972), pp. 1-8.

6. "The Early History of the Titius-Bode Law," *American Journal of Physics* 40 (1972), pp. 1014-1023.

7. "Brain, Mind and Computers," *Journal of the American Scientific Affiliation* 24 (1972), pp. 12-17.

8. "No Other Options," *Journal of the American Scientific Affiliation* 24 (1972), p. 127.

9. "The Titius-Bode Law: A Strange Bicentenary," *Sky and Telescope* 43 (1972), pp. 280-281.

10. Review of P. T Gunter (ed. and trans.), *Bergson and the Evolution of Physics* (Knoxville, Tenn.: University of Tennessee Press, 1969), in *Zygon* 7 (1972), pp. 138-139.

1973

1. "God and Creation: A Biblical-Scientific Reflection," *Theology Today* 30 (1973), pp. 111-120.

2. "Science morale et éthique scientifique," *Cahier bilingue de l'Association Lecomte de Nouy* (Spring 1973), pp. 15-30.

3. "Ethical Science and Scientific Ethics," English version of 1973(2) in *Cahier bilingue de l'Association Lecomte de Nouy* (Spring 1973), pp. 47-61.

4. "The Last Century of Science: Progress, Problems and Prospects," *Proceedings of the Second International Humanistic Symposium* (Athens: Hellenic Society for Humanistic Studies 1973), pp. 248-264.

5. Review of M. N. Richter, *Science as a Cultural Process* (Cambridge, Mass.: Schenken Publishing Company, 1972) in *Isis* 64 (1973), p. 544.

6. Review of L. S. Swenson, Jr. *The Ethereal Aether: A History of the Michelson-Morley-Miller Aether-Drift Experiments 1880-1930* (Austin, Texas: University of Texas Press, 1972) in *American Scientist* (January-February 1973), p. 104.

7. Articles in *The McGraw-Hill Encyclopedia of World Biography* (New York: McGraw-Hill Book Company, 1973) on the following scientists:

Ampère 1:164-165	Fresnel 4:233-234
Becquerel 1:453-454	Galileo 4:289-292
Bohr 2:44-47	Hamilton 5:62-64
Boltzmnn 2:52-54	Helmholtz 5:177-179
Born 2:82-83	Hertz 5:243-244
Bothe 2:100-101	Joliot-Curie 6:50
Brahe 2:140-141	Kepler 6:176-179
Carnot, S. 2:380-381	Kirchoff 6:214-215.
Chadwick 2:459-460	Lorentz 6:568-569.
Clausius 3:25-26	Napier 8:61-62.
Cockcroft 3:61-62	Oersted 8:183-185.

Copernicus 3:61-62
Curie, M. 3:213-215
Debye 3:213-215
Dirac 3:389-390
Fizeau 4:131
Fourier 4:173
Fraunhofer 4:207-208

Ohm 8:191-192.
Regiomontanus 9:133-134.
Roentgen 9:247-249.
Vesalius 11:132-133.
van der Waals 11:197-198.
Wigner 11:357-358.
Wilson, C. 11:397-398.

1974

1. *Science and Creation: From Eternal Cycles to an Oscillating Universe* (Edinburgh: Scottish Academic Press 1974), 367pp.

2. "Scientific Ethics and Ethical Science," in *Philosophy and Humanistic Literature: Three Scientific Communications* (Athens: Hellenic Society for Humanistic Studies, 1974)), pp. 39-53.

3. "The Better Part of Kohoutek," *Hallmark News* (Seton Hall University, South Orange, N. J.) 5 (Spring 1974), pp. 4-5.

1975

1. Translation from the Italian, with an Introduction and notes, of Giordano Bruno, *The Ash Wednesday Supper* (The Hague: Mouton, 1975), 174pp.

2. *The Milky Way: An Elusive Road for Science*, paperback reprint of 1972(1) (New York: Science History Publications, 1975).

3. "A Hundred Years of Two Cultures," *The University of Windsor Review* 11 (1975), pp. 55-59.

4. "Knowledge in an Age of Science," *The University of Windsor Review* 11 (1975), pp. 80-103.

5. *Culture and Science*, reprint with new pagination of 1975(3) and (4). (Windsor, Canada: University of Windsor Press, 1975), 52pp.

6. "The Edge of Precision," reprint of 1966(1), pp. 273-279, in John F. Hanahan (ed.), *The Ascent of Man: Sources and Interpretations* (Boston: Little, Brown and Company, 1975), pp. 257-262.

7. Review of N. R. Hanson, *Constellations and Conjectures*, W. C. Humphreys, Jr. (ed.) (Dordrecht: D. Reidel, 1973) in *Isis* 66 (1975), pp. 110-112.

1976

1. Translation from the German, with an Introduction and notes, of J. H. Lambert, *Cosmological Letters on the Arrangement of the World-Edifice* (New York: Science History Publications, 1976), 245pp.

2. "Theological Aspects of Creative Science," in W. A. McKinney (ed.), *Creation, Christ and Culture: Studies in Honour of T. F. Torrance* (Edinburgh: T. & T. Clark, 1976), pp. 149-166.

3. "Von subjektiven Wissenschaftlern zur objektiven Wissenschaft," German translation of 1977(1), in W. Becker and K. Hübner (eds.), *Objectivität in den Naturwissenschaften* (Hamburg: Hoffman and Campe, 1976), pp. 154-168.

4. "The Five Forms of Laplace's Cosmogony," *American Journal of Physics* 44 (1976), pp. 4-11.

5. Review of F. Ferré, *Shaping the Future: Resources of the Post Modern World* (New York: Harper and Row, 1976) in *Theology Today* 33 (1976), pp. 315-317.

1977

1. "From Subjective Scientists to Objective Science," in *Proceedings of the Third International Humanistic Symposium* (Athens: Hellenic Society for Humanistic Studies, 1977), pp. 314-336.

2. "Lambert: Self-taught Physicist," *Physics Today* 30 (September 1977), pp. 25-32.

3. "Dunkle Regenten als Vorläufer schwarzer Löcher," *Nachrichten der Olbers Gesellschaft* 107 (December 1977), pp. 3-10.

4. "The History of Science and the Idea of an Oscillating Universe," in W. Yourgrau and A. D. Breck (eds.), *Cosmology, History and Theology.* (New York: Plenum Press, 1977), pp. 233-251.

5. "An English translation of the Third Part of Kant's *Universal Natural History and Theory of the Heavens,*" in W. Yourgrau and A. D. Breck (eds.), *Cosmology, History and Theology* (New York: Plenum Press, 1977), pp. 387-403.

1978

1. *Planets and Planetarians: A History of Theories of the Origin of Planetary Systems* (Edinburgh: Scottish Academic Press; New York: The Halstead Press of John Wiley Inc., 1978), vi + 266pp, with 42 illustrations.

2. *The Road of Science and the Ways to God: The Gifford Lectures 1975 and 1976* (Chicago: University of Chicago Press; Edinburgh: Scottish Academic Press, 1978), 475pp.

3. *Brain, Mind and Computers,* reprint with a new Introduction of 1969(1) (South Bend, Ind.: Gateway Editions, 1978), 267pp.

4. *And on This Rock: The Witness of One Land and Two Covenants* (Notre Dame, Ind.: Ave Maria Press, 1978), 128pp.

5. *The Origin of Science and the Science of its Origin* (Edinburgh: Scottish Academic Press; South Bend, Ind.: Gateway Editions, 1978), 160pp.

6. "Decision-Making in Business: Amoral?" in *Trends in Business and Ethics.* Nijenrode Studies in Business 3 (Leiden: Martinus Nijhoff, 1978), pp. 1-10.

7. "Ethics and the Science of Decision-Making in Business: A Specification of Perspectives," in *Trends in Business and Ethics.* Nijenrode Studies in Business 3 (Leiden: Martinus Nijhoff, 1978), pp. 141-156.

8. "The Chaos of Scientific Cosmology," in D. Huff and O. Prewett (eds.), *The Nature of the Physical Universe: 1976 Nobel Conference* (New York: John Wiley, 1978), pp. 83-112.

9. "A Forgotten Bicentenary: Johann Georg von Soldner," *Sky and Telescope* 6 (June 1978), pp. 460-461.

10. "Johann Georg von Soldner and the Gravitational Bending of Light. With an English translation of his Essay on it published in 1801," *Foundations of Physics* 8 (1978), pp. 927-950.

11. "Lambert and the Watershed of Cosmology," *Scientia* (Milano) 113 (1978), pp. 75-95.

12. "Lambert e lo spartiacque della cosmologia," Italian translation of 1978(11), *Scientia* (Milano) 113 (1978), pp. 97-114.

13. "The Metaphysics of Discovery and the Rediscovery of Metaphysics," *Proceedings of the American Catholic Philosophical Association* 52 (1978), pp. 188-196.

14. Review of H. Schwarz, *Our Cosmic Journey: Christian Anthropology in the Light of Current Trends in the Sciences, Philosophy, and Theology* (Minneapolis, Minn.: Augsburg, 1977) in *Theology Today*, 35 (1978) pp. 360-362.

15. "Paradoxes in Cosmology," *Cahiers Fundamenta Scientiae* (Stras-bourg) 82 (1978), pp. 33-36.

1979

1. "Das Gravitations-Paradoxon des unendlichen Universums," *Südhoffs Archiv* 63 (1979), pp. 105-122. English version in 1990(24).

2. "The Reality Beneath: The World View of Rutherford," in M. Bunge and W. R. Shea (eds.), *Rutherford and Physics at the Turn of the Century* (New York: Dawson and Science History Publications, 1979), pp. 110-123.

3. "The Forces and Powers of Nature," *Theology Today* 36 (1979), pp. 87-91.

4. "Sur l'édition et la reédition de la traduction française des *Cosmologische Briefe* de Lambert," *Revue d'Histoire des Sciences* 32 (1979), pp. 305-314.

5. "The Cosmological Letters of Lambert and His Cosmology," *Colloque International Jean-Henri Lambert (1728-1777)* (Paris: Editions Ophrys, 1979), pp. 291–300.

6. "'And on This Rock . . .' Divine Origin of the Papacy," *The Wanderer* (December 13, 1979), pp. 1 and 6.

7. "Science and Christian Theism: A Mutual Witness," *Scottish Journal of Theology* 32 (1979), pp. 563–570.

8. Review of H. Reichenbach, *Selected Writings, 1909-1953*, M. Reichenbach and R. S. Cohen (eds.) (Dordrecht: Reidel, 1979) in *Nature* 282 (November 1, 1979), pp. 114–115.

9. Review of E. M. Klaaren, *Religious Origins of Modern Science: Belief in Creation in Seventeenth-Century Thought* (Grand Rapids, Mich.: Eerdman, 1977) in *Theology Today* 35 (1979), pp. 496–497.

10. Review of R. Jaquel, *Le savant mulhousien Jean-Henri Lambert (1728-1777): Etudes critiques et documentaires* (Paris: Editions Ophrys, 1977) in *Isis* 70 (1979), p. 178.

1980

1. *Cosmos and Creator* (Edinburgh: Scottish Academic Press, 1980), xii + 168pp.

2. *The Road of Science and the Ways to God*, Phoenix Paperback reprint of 1978(2).

3. Review of A. R. Peacocke, *Creation and the World of Science: The Bampton Lectures 1978* (Oxford: Clarendon Press, 1979) in *Nature* 284 (24 April 1980), pp. 667–668.

4. Review of G. Tauber, *Man's View of the Universe. A Pictorial History: Evolving Concepts of the Universe from Ancient Times to Today's Space Probes* (New York: Crown Publishers, 1979) in *Isis* 71 (1980), p. 668.

5. "'And on This Rock . . .' Divine Origin of the Papacy," reprint, by the Wanderer Press, in brochure with new Foreword, of 1979(6).

6. "A Brief Reminiscence," in *Henry Francis Regnery, 1945-1979: In Memoriam* (Three Oaks, Mich.: 1980), p. 91.

1981

1. Translation, with Introduction and notes, of Immanuel Kant, *Universal Natural History and Theory of the Heavens* (Edinburgh: Scottish Academic Press, 1981), 302pp.

2. *Cosmos and Creator*, American publication of 1980(1) (Chicago: Gateway Editions, 1981).

3. "Chance or Reality: Interaction in Nature versus Measurement in Physics," *Philosophia* (Athens) 10-11 (1980-1981), pp. 85-105.

4. "De la science-fiction à la philosophie," in *Science et antiscience*. Collection: Recherches et débats (Paris: Centurion, 1981), pp. 37-51.

5. "Lo absoluto bajo lo relativo: Unas reflexiones sobre las teorias de Einstein," *Anuario Filosofico* (Pamplona: Universidad de Navarra) 14/1 (1981), pp. 41-62.

6. "Religion and Science: The Cosmic Connection," in J. A. Howard (ed.), *Belief, Faith and Reason* (Belfast: Christian Journals, 1981), pp. 11-28.

7. "The Business of Christianity and the Christianity of Business," *Conference on World Religions and Business Behavior. Documents* (Nijenrode, The Netherlands: The Netherlands School of Business, 1981), pp. 206-229.

8. Author's Abstract of *The Road of Science and the Ways to God* 1978(2), *The Monist* 64 (1981), p. 126.

9. Author's Abstract of *Cosmos and Creator* 1980(1) and 1981(2), *The Monist* 64 (1981), p. 420.

10. "Il caos della cosmologia scientifica," Italian translation of 1978(8) in D. Huff and O. Prewett (eds.), *La natura dell'universo fisico* (Torino: P. Boringhieri, 1981), pp. 88-114.

1982

1. "The University and the Universe," in J. R. Wilburn (ed.), *Freedom, Order and the University* (Malibu, Ca.: Pepperdine University Press, 1982), pp. 43-68.

2. "Il caso o la realtà," Italian translation of 1981(3), *Il Nuovo Areopago* 1/2 (1982), pp. 28-48.

3. "Zufall oder Realität," German translation of 1981(3), *Philosophia naturalis* 19 (1982), pp. 498-518.

4. "From Scientific Cosmology to a Created Universe," *Irish Astronomical Journal* 15 (1982), pp. 253-262.

5. Author's Abstract of *Universal Natural History* 1981(1), *The Monist* 65 (1982), p. 281.

1983

1. *Et sur ce Roc: Témoignage d'une terre et de deux testaments,* French translation of 1978(4) (Paris: Téqui, 1983), 111pp.

2. *Angels, Apes and Men* (La Salle, Ill.: Sherwood Sugden and Company, 1983), 128pp.

3. "The Wronging of Wright," in A. Van der Merwe (ed.), *Old and New Questions in Physics, Cosmology, Philosophy and Theoretical Biology. Essays in Honor of Wolfgang Yourgrau* (New York: Plenum, 1983), pp. 593-605.

4. "E su questa pietra . . .," Italian translation of pp. 45-52 and 93-102 of 1978(4), *Il Nuovo Areopago* 2/4 (1983), pp. 197-214.

5. "The Greeks of Old and the Novelty of Science," *Arete Mneme: Konst Vourveris. Vourveris Festschrift* (Athens: Hellenic Humanistic Society, 1983), pp. 263-277.

6. "The Physics of Impetus and the Impetus of the Kuran," *International Conference on Science in Islamic Polity -- Its Past, Present and Future: Abstract*

of Papers, 19-24 November 1983, Islamabad (Islamabad: Ministry of Science and Technology, Government of Pakistan and Organisation of Islamic Conference, 1983), pp. 36-37. For full text see 1985(7).

7. "Cosmology as Philosophy," *16. Weltkongress für Philosophie 1978* (Frankfurt: a. M./Bern; New York: Peter Lang, 1983), pp. 149-154.

1984

1. *Uneasy Genius: The Life and Work of Pierre Duhem* (Dordrecht: Martinus Nijhoff, 1984), xii + 472pp.

2. "Maritain and Science," *The New Scholasticism* 58 (1984), pp. 267-292.

3. "Chesterton's Landmark Year: The Blatchford-Chesterton Debate of 1903-1904," *The Chesterton Review* 10 (1984), pp. 409-423.

4. "God and Man's Science: A View of Creation," *Christian Vision: Man in Society* (Hillsdale, Mich.: Hillsdale College Press, 1984), pp. 35-49.

5. "The Creator's Coming," *Homiletic and Pastoral Review* 85 (December 1984), pp. 10-15.

6. Introduction to E. Gilson, *From Aristotle to Darwin and Back Again*, trans. J. Lyon (Notre Dame, Ind.: University of Notre Dame Press, 1984), pp. xii-xviii.

7. "From Scientific Cosmology to a Created Universe," reprint of 1982(4) in R. A. Varghese (ed.). *The Intellectuals Speak out about God.* (Chicago: Regnery-Gateway, 1984), pp. 61-78.

8. "An Author's Reflections," *The Dawson Newsletter* 3 (Summer 1984), pp. 6-8.

9. "The History of Science and the Idea of an Oscillating Universe," reprint of 1977(4) with a new postscript, *The Center Journal*, 4 (1984) pp. 131-165.

10. Review of P. Redondi, *Epistemologia e storia della scienza. Le svolte teoriche da Duhem a Bachelard* (Milano: Feltrinelli, 1978) in *Revue d'Histoire des Sciences* 37 (1984), pp. 85-87.

11. Review of A. R. Peacocke (ed.), *The Sciences and Theology.* (Stocksfield: Oriel Press, 1984) in *The Heythrop Journal* 25 (1984), pp. 391-393.

12. Review of L. Bouyer, *Cosmos et la gloire de Dieu* (Paris: Cerf, 1982) in *The Downside Review* 102 (1984), pp. 301-307.

13. Review of P. Bowler, *The Eclipse of Darwinism: Anti Darwinian Theories in the Decades around 1900* (Baltimore, Md.: Johns Hopkins Press, 1983) in *The Tablet* 238 (February 11, 1984), pp. 135-136.

14. "Scientists on Science and God," review of F. Hoyle, *The Intelligent Universe* (New York: Holt, Rinehart and Winston, 1984); Sir John Eccles and D. Robinson, *The Wonder of Being Human: Our Brain and Our Mind* (New York: The Free Press, 1984); P. Davies, *Superforce: The Search for a Grand Unified Theory of Nature* (New York: Simon and Schuster, 1984) in *Reflections (The Wanderer Review of Literature, Culture and the Arts)* 3 (Fall 1984), p. 9.

15. Review of V. Long, *Upon This Rock* (Chicago: Franciscan Herald Press, 1983) *Reflections* 4 (Winter 1984), p. 20.

1985

1. *Angels, Apes and Men*, reprint of 1983(2).

2. Introductory Essay to Pierre Duhem, *To Save the Phenomena*, paperback reprint of 1969(4).

3. "The Absolute Beneath the Relative: Reflections on Einstein's Theories," English version of 1981(5), *Intercollegiate Review* 20 (Spring/Summer 1985), pp. 29-38.

4. "Christ, Catholics and Abortion," *Homiletic and Pastoral Review* 85 (March 1985), pp. 7-15.

5. "The Creator's Coming," reprint of 1984(5), *Faith Magazine* 17/3 (1985), pp. 10-14.

6. "On Whose Side is History?" *National Review* (23 August 1985), pp. 41-47.

7. "The Physics of Impetus and the Impetus of the Koran," *Modern Age* 29 (1985), pp. 153-160.

8. "Chance or Reality," reprint of 1982(2), *Freiheit und Notwendigkeit in der Europäischen Zivilisation: Perspectiven des modernen Bewusstseins. Referate und Texte des 5. Internationalen Humanistischen Symposiums 1981* (Athens: Hellenic Humanistic Society, 1985), pp. 303-322.

9. "Christian Culture and Duhem's Work," reprint of 1984(8), *Downside Review* 103 (1985), pp. 137-143.

10. Review of J. Polkinghorne, *The Way the World Is* (Grand Rapids, Mich.: Eerdmans, 1984, in *National Review* (22 March 1985), pp. 53-55.

11. Review of P. B. Medawar, *The Limits of Science* (New York: Harper and Row, 1984) in *Reflections* 5/1 (Winter 1985) p. 9.

12. "Creation and Monastic Creativity," *Monastic Studies* (Toronto) 16 (Christmas 1985) pp. 79-92.

13. "The Teacher: Dr. Victor Hess. The Student: Rev. Stanley Jaki," *Fordham* (New York), (Fall 1985), pp. 10-11.

14. Foreword to Pierre Duhem, *Medieval Cosmology: Theories of Infinity, Place, Time, Void and the Plurality of Worlds*, R. Ariew (ed. and trans.), (Chicago: University Press, 1985), pp. xi-xviii.

15. "Science and Hope," *The Hillsdale Review* 7/2 (1985), pp. 3-16.

16. "Dawson and the New Age," review of C. Dawson, *Christianity and the New Age*, reprinted with an Introduction by John J. Mulloy (Manchester, N.H.: Sophia Institute Press, 1985) in *The Hillsdale Review* 7/3 (1985), pp. 57-60.

1986

1. *Science and Creation*, reprint with a postscript of 1974(1), 377pp.

2. *Lord Gifford and His Lectures: A Centenary Retrospect* (Edinburgh: Scottish Academic Press, 1986; Macon, Georgia: Mercer University Press, 1986), 138pp.

3. *The Keys of the Kingdom: A Tool's Witness to Truth* (Chicago: The Franciscan Herald Press, 1986), 226pp.

4. *Chesterton: A Seer of Science* (Urbana: University of Illinois Press, 1986), x + 164pp.

5. *Chance or Reality and Other Essays* (Lanham, Md and London: University Press of America; Bryn Mawr, Pa.: The Intercollegiate Studies Inc., 1986), viii + 250pp; reprint of 1967(2), 1969(3), 1975(3), 1975(4), 1976(2), 1977(1), 1981(3), 1982(1), 1983(5), 1984(2), 1984(3), 1984(8), 1985(6).

6. "Order in Nature and Society: Open or Specific," in G. W. Carey (ed.), *Order, Freedom and the Polity (Critical Essays on the Open Society)* (Lanham, Md. and London: University Press of America; Bryn Mawr, Pa.: The Intercollegiate Studies Institute, 1986), pp. 91-111.

7. "Man of One Wife or Celibacy," *Homiletic and Pastoral Review* 87/4 (January 1986), pp. 18-25.

8. "Un siècle de Gifford Lectures," French translation of Chapter 1 of 1986(2), *Archives de Philosophie* 49 (1986), pp. 3-49.

9. "The Case for Galileo's Rehabilitation," *Fidelity* 5 (March 1986), pp. 37-41.

10. "A Most Holy Night," review of R. Laurentin, *The Truth of Christmas Beyond the Myths: The Infancy Narratives of Christ* (Petersham, Mass.: St. Bede's Publications, 1986) in *Reflections* 5 (Summer 1986), pp. 1 and 21.

11. "Cosmic Stakes," review of J. D. Barrow and F. J. Tipler, *The Anthropic Cosmological Principle* (New York: Oxford University Press,

1986); J. D. Barrow and J. Silk, *The Origin and Evolution of the Expanding Universe* (New York: Basic Books, 1983); and H. R. Pagels, *Perfect Symmetry: The Search for the Beginning of Time* (New York: Simon and Schuster, 1985) in *Reflections* 5 (Summer 1986), p. 8.

12. "Monkeys and Machine-Guns: Evolution, Darwinism and Christianity," *Chronicles* 10 (August 1986), pp. 15-18.

13. "The Intelligent Christian's Guide to Scientific Cosmology, or Intelligence and Cosmology," *Faith and Reason* 12 (1986), pp. 124-136.

14. "Science and Censorship: Hélène Duhem and the Publication of the *Système du monde*," *Intercollegiate Review* 21 (Winter 1985-1986), pp. 41-49.

15. "The Impasse of Planck's Epistemology," *Philosophia* (Athens) 15-16 (1985-1986), pp. 467-489.

16. "Science for Catholics," *The Dawson Newsletter* 5 (Winter 86-87), pp. 5-11.

17. "Das Weltall als Zufall - ein Mythos von kosmischer Irrationalität," in H. Lenk *et al.* (eds.), *Zur Kritik der Wissenschaftlichen Rationalität* (Freiburg: Verlag Karl Alber, 1986), pp. 487-503.

18. "G. K. C. as R. C." *Faith and Reason* 12 (1986), pp. 211-228.

1987

1. *And on This Rock: The Witness of One Land and Two Covenants*, second edition, revised and enlarged of 1978(4) (Manassas, Va: Trinity Communications, 1987), 128pp.

2. *Uneasy Genius: The Life and Work of Pierre Duhem*, second (paperback) edition of 1984(1).

3. Edition with introduction in English of early essays on the history and philosophy of physics by Pierre Duhem, *Prémices philosophiques* (Leiden: E. J. Brill, 1987), xiii + 239pp.

4. "Address on receiving the Templeton Prize," (Nassau, Bahamas: Lismore Press, 1987), pp. 14-17.

5. "Miracles and Physics," *The Asbury Theological Journal* 42 (1987), pp. 5-42.

6. "Teaching Transcendence in Physics," *American Journal of Physics* 55 (October 1987), pp. 884-888.

7. "Religion and Science," *The World Encyclopaedia of Religions* (New York: Macmillan, 1987), vol. 13, pp. 121-133.

8. "A Theologian and Scientist Talks about Creator and Church," interview with M. L. Mudde, *The Wanderer* (August 13, 1987), p. 3.

9. "Newman's Logic and the Logic of the Papacy," *Faith and Reason* 13 (1987), pp. 241-265.

10. "Scienza, Dio, Progresso," in R. Barbieri (ed.), *Uomini e Tempo Moderno* (Milano: Jaca Book, 1987), pp. 181-183.

11. "Maritain and Science," in D. W. Hudson and M. J. Mancini (eds.), *Understanding Maritain: Philosopher and Friend* (Macon, Ga: Mercer University Press, 1987), pp. 183-200; reprint of 1984(2).

12. "Le physicien et le métaphysicien. La correspondance entre Pierre Duhem et Réginald Garrigou-Lagrange," *Actes de l'Académie Nationale des Sciences, Belles-Lettres et Arts de Bordeaux* 12 (1987), pp. 93-116.

13. "The Modernity of the Middle Ages," *Modern Age* 31 (Summer/ Fall 1987), pp. 207-214.

14. "Normalcy as Terror. The Naturalization of AIDS," *Crisis* 5/6 (1987), pp. 21-23.

15. "Science: From the Womb of Religion," *The Christian Century* 104/28 (1987), pp. 851-854; reprint of 1987(4).

16. "'Hit, Tudomány, Haladás," *Vigilia* (Budapest) 52/8 (1987), pp. 620-624; Hungarian translation of 1987(4).

17. "El hambre basica de la humanidad," *Nuestro Tiempo* (Madrid) 71 (October 1987), pp. 48–61; Spanish translation of 1987(4).

18. "The Absolute beneath the Relative: Reflections on Einstein's Theories," in *Einstein and the Humanities*, ed. D. P. Ryan (New York: Greenwood Press, 1987), pp. 5–18; reprint of 1985(3).

1988

1. *The Savior of Science* (Washington, D. C.: Regnery Gateway, 1988), 268pp.

2. *The Absolute Beneath the Relative* (Lanham, Md. and London: University Press of America; Bryn Mawr, Pa.: Intercollegiate Studies Institute, 1988), 233pp; reprint of 1972(7), 1973(4), 1974(2), 1978(13), 1984(4), 1985(3), 1985(7), 1985(14), 1985(15), 1986(6), 1986(12), 1986(14), and two hitherto unpublished essays listed below as 1988(17) and 1988(18).

3. *The Physicist As Artist: The Landscapes of Pierre Duhem* (Edinburgh: Scottish Academic Press, 1988), 188pp in 4° (Introduction with 235 illustrations in half tone and ten color plates).

4. *La strada della scienza e le vie verso Dio,* Italian translation of 1978(2) (Milano: Jaca Book, 1988), 482pp.

5. "Bible, Science, Church," review of C. A. Russell, *Cross-Currents: Interactions between Science and Faith* (Grand Rapids, Michigan: Wm. B. Eerdmans Publishing Co., 1985) in *Reflections* 7/1 (Winter 1988), p. 2.

6. "The Universe in the Bible and in Modern Science," in *Ex Auditu Volume III* (Pittsburgh: Pickwick Publications, 1988), pp. 137–147.

7. "The Three Faces of Technology: Idol, Nemesis, Marvel," *The Intercollegiate Review* 23/2 (Spring 1988), pp. 37–46.

8. "Physics and the Ultimate," *Ultimate Reality and Meaning* 11 (March 1988), pp. 61–73.

9. "Evicting the Creator," review of S. W. Hawking, *A Brief History of Time. From the Big Bang to Black Holes* (New York: Bantam Books, 1988) in *Reflections* 7 (Spring 1988), pp. 1, 20, 22.

10. "Big Bang di errori," review of S. W. Hawking, *Dal Big Bang ai buchi neri. Brevi storia del tempo* (Milano: Rizzoli, 1988) in *Il Sabato* (15–21 ottobre 1988), pp. 33–34. Abbreviated Italian version of 1988(9).

11. "Language, Logic, Logos," *The Asbury Theological Journal* 43/2 (1988), pp. 95–136.

12. "La science: enjeu idéologique," interview in *L'Homme Nouveau* (August 7-21, 1988), p. 4.

13. "The Only Chaos," *This World* 22 (Summer 1988), pp. 99–109.

14. "The Role of Faith in Physics," reprint of 1967(2) in W. C. Booth and M. W. Gregory (eds.), *The Harper and Row Reader. Liberal Education Through Reading and Writing* (New York: Harper and Row, 1988), pp. 648-663.

15. "Monos y metralletas: evolución, darwinismo y cristianismo," *Nuestro Tiempo* 75 (Mayo 1988), pp. 116-123, Spanish translation of 1986(12).

16. "Address on receiving the Templeton Prize," reprint of 1987(4) in *The Templeton Foundation Prize for Progress in Religion*, ed. W. Forker (Edinburgh: Scottish Academic Press, 1988), pp. 208-218.

17. "The Role of Physics in Psychology: The Prospects in Retrospect," in 1988(2), pp. 85-101.

18. "The Demythologization of Science," in 1988(2), pp. 198-213.

1989

1. *God and the Cosmologists* (Washington, D.C.: Regnery Gateway; Edinburgh: Scottish Academic Press, 1989), 286pp.

2. *Miracles and Physics* (Front Royal, Va.: Christendom Press, 1989), 114pp; reprint with an Introduction and minor changes of 1987(5).

3. *Brain, Mind and Computers* (Washington, D.C.: Gateway Editions, 1989), 316pp; reprint with a new Foreword of 1978(3) and 1988(11).

4. "Science: Revolutionary or Conservative?" *The Intercollegiate Review* 24 (Spring 1989), pp. 13-22.

5. Introduction to P. Duhem, *Au pays des gorilles* (Paris: Beauchesne, 1989), pp. iii-xi.

6. "The Physicist and the Metaphysician," *The New Scholasticism* 63 (1989), pp. 183-205; English version of 1987(12).

7. "Meditations on Newman's *Grammar of Assent,*" *Faith and Reason* 15 (1989), pp. 19-34.

8. Contributions to *Meeting '88. Cercatori di Infinito. Costruttori di Storia* (Rimini: 1989), pp. 55-57, 62-63, 203-204.

9. Introduction to S. L. Jaki (ed.), *Newman Today* (The Proceedings of the Wethersfield Institute, Volume 1, 1988) (San Francisco: Ignatius Press, 1989), pp. 7-16.

10. "Newman's Assent to Reality, Natural and Supernatural," in S. L. Jaki (ed.), *Newman Today*, pp. 189-220.

11. "L'assoluto al di là del relativo: riflessioni sulle teorie di Einstein," *Communio* 103 (Jan-Feb 1989), pp. 103-109; Italian translation of 1972(7).

12. "Thomas and the Universe," *The Thomist* 53 (1989), pp. 545-572.

13. "The Virgin Birth and the Birth of Science," *The Downside Review* 107 (1989), pp. 255-273, with five illustrations.

14. "Evicting the Creator," reprint of 1988(9) in *Science and Religion Forum. Reviews* 14 (May 1989), pp. 5-16.

15. "Cosmologia e religione," *Synesis* 6/4 (1989), pp. 89-100; Italian translation of 1990(26).

1990

1. *The Purpose of It All* (Washington, D.C.: Regnery Gateway; Edinburgh: Scottish Academic Press, 1990), 297pp

2. *The Only Chaos and Other Essays* (Lanham, Md.: University Press of America; Bryn Mawr, Pa.: Intercollegiate Studies Institute, 1990), reprint, with a new Introduction, of 1988(13), 1987(13), 1984(9), 1989(4), 1988(7), 1987(14), 1988(9), 1987(6), 1988(8), 1988(6), 1987(4) and first publication of 1990(14), 1990(15), 1990(16), 1990(17), 1990(18), 1990(19).

3. *Catholic Essays* (Front Royal, Va.: Christendom Press, 1990), reprint, with an Introduction, of 1986(14), 1986(9), 1984(5), 1986(10), 1985(4), 1986(7), 1986(18), 1981(7), 1986(13), and first publication of 1990(20).

4. *Cosmos in Transition: Essays in the History of Cosmology* (Tucson, Arizona: Pachart, Publishing House, 1990), reprint, with an Introduction, of 1971(1), 1972(4), 1978(11), 1983(3), 1976(4), 1972(6), 1978(10), 1978(8) and 1990(24).

5. *The Savior of Science* (Edinburgh: Scottish Academic Press, 1990), UK edition of 1988(1).

6. *A Tudomány Megváltója* (Budapest: Ecclesia, 1990), 278pp, Hungarian translation by Kinga Scholtz of 1988(1).

7. *Science and Creation: From Eternal Cycles to an Oscillating Universe* (Lanham, Md.: University Press of America, 1990), American edition of 1986(1).

8. *Ciencia, Fe, Cultura* (Madrid: Libros MC, 1990), 208pp, Spanish translation by Ana Artigas, with an Introductory essay ("La Obra de Stanley L. Jaki") by M. Artigas, of 1975(3), 1975(4), 1977(1), 1967(2), 1976(2), 1974(2), 1988(15).

9. "Socrates, or the Baby and the Bathwater," *Faith and Reason* 16 (1990), pp. 63-79.

10. "Determinism and Reality," *Great Ideas Today 1990* (Chicago: Encyclopedia Britannica, 1990), pp. 277-302.

11. "Science and the Future of Religion," *Modern Age* 33 (Summer 1990), pp. 142-150.

12. "Christology and the Birth of Science," *Asbury Thelogical Journal* 45/2 (1990), pp. 61-72.

13. "Cosmology and Religion," *Philosophy in Science*, Volume 4 (1990), pp. 47-81,

14. "The Cosmic Myth of Chance," English original of 1986(17) in 1990(2), pp. 17-30.

15. "The Transformation of Cosmology in the Renaissance," in 1990(2), pp. 64-62.

16. "Extra-terrestrials and Scientific Progress," in 1990(2), pp. 92-103.

17. "Physics or Physicalism: A Cultural Dilemma," in 1990(2), pp. 162-178.

18. "Science and Antiscience," revised English original of 1981(4), in 1990(2), pp. 179-200.

19. "The Hymn of the Universe," in 1990(2), pp. 233-245.

20. "Commencement," in 1990(3), pp. 166-176.

21. "Pierre Duhem: Physicien et paysagiste," in *Colloque Pierre Duhem (1861 - 1916). Scientifique, Ancien Elève de Stanislas. Samedi 3 Décembre - Dimanche 4 Décembre 1988. Actes du Colloque* (Paris: Stanislas. Classes Préparatoires, [1990]), pp. 47-54.

22. "Katolikus Tudomány," *Vigilia* (Budapest) 55 (March 1990), pp. 168-174; Hungarian translation of 1986(16).

23. "Krisztológia as a modern tudomány születése," *Jel* ["Sign"] (Budapest) 2/5 (1990), pp. 7-12; Hungarian translation of 1990(12).

24. "The Gravitational Paradox of an Infinite Universe," English original of 1979(1) in 1990(4).

25. "The Virgin Birth and the Birth of Science," reprint in booklet form (Front Royal, Va.: Christendom Press, 1990), 32 pp., of 1989(13), with five illustrations in color.

26. "Cosmology and Religion," *Athéisme et Foi* 25/3 (Città del Vaticano: Pontificium Consilium pro dialogo cum non credentibus, 1990), pp. 252–265, English original of 1989(15).

27. "Newman and Science," *Downside Review* 108 (1990), pp. 282–294.

28. Review of D. L. Sepper, *Goethe contra Newton: Polemics and the Project for a New Science* (New York: Cambridge University Press, 1988) in *American Historical Review* 95 (1990), pp. 1492–1493.

29. Introduction to E. Gilson, *Methodical Realism* (Front Royal, Va.: Christendom Press, 1990), tr. P. Trower.

30. "A modern tudományos kozmológia és a kozmológiai istenérv," JEL 2/6 (1990), pp. 9–17; Hungarian translation of 1990(13).

31. "La cristologia e la nascita della scienza moderna," *Annales theologici* 4/2 (1990), pp. 334–348; Italian translation of 1990(12).

32. "Sushchestvnet li Sozdatel?" ["Does a Creator Exist?"] in *Obsh-chest-vennye nauki Akademiia nauk SSSR* [Moscow] 6 (1990), pp. 170–180; Russian translation of a lecture delivered in English in Moscow, June 22, 1989.

33. "La fisica all ricerca di una realtà ultima," *Cultura e Libri* (Maggio-Giugno, 1990), pp. 21–41; Italian translation of 1988(8).

1991

1. *Pierre Duhem: Scientist and Catholic* (Front Royal, Va.: Christendom Press, 1991), 204pp.

2. *Pierre Duhem: Homme de science et de foi,* tr. F. Raymondaud (Paris: Beauchesne, 1991), 275pp, French translation of 1991(1).

3. *Olbers Studies: With Three Unpublished Manuscripts by Olbers* (Tucson, Arizona: Pachart Publishing House, 1991), 96pp, publication in English of 1970(1), 1970(2), 1970(3) and reprint of 1970(4).

4. *Erre a sziklára* (Budapest: Ecclesia, 1991), 156pp; Hungarian translation by Z. Jaki and C. Schilly of 1987(1)

5. "A Teremtő kilakoltatása," JEL 3/1 (1991), pp. 5-7; Hungarian translation of 1988(9).

6. "The Mind: Its Physics or Physiognomy," a review of R. Penrose, *The Emperor's New Mind: Concerning Computers, Minds, and the Laws of Physics* (Cambridge: University Press, 1989), 480pp., in *Reflections* 10/2 (1991), pp. 1, 14-15. Also in *Science and Religion Forum. Reviews* (February 1991), pp. 9-16.

7. "Newman and Evolution," *The Downside Review* 109 (January 1991), pp. 16-34.

8. "Los científicos y la filosifía," interview in *Atlántida* (enero–marzo 1991), pp. 76-82.

9. "An Interview with Dr. Stanley Jaki," *The Observer of Boston College* 9 (April/May 1991), pp. 12-13 and 17 in 4°. English text of 1991(8).

10. Commencement Address. Christendom College, May 12, 1991 (Front Royal, Va.: Christendom Press), a brochure of 16pp.

11. "Beyond the Tools of Production," pp. 5-7 in "Reflections on the 100th Anniversary of *Rerum Novarum*," a *Wanderer Supplement*, May 16, 1991.

12. "Krisztus, a katolikusok és az abortusz" JEL 3/3 (1991), pp. 70-74; Hungarian translation of 1985(4)

13. *Az ország kulcsai: Egy eszköz tanúságtétele* (Budapest: Ecclesia, 1991), in press; Hungarian translation of 1986(3)

14. *Dio e i cosmologi* (Città del Vaticano: Libreria Editrice Vaticana, 1991), in press; Italian translation by Maria Luisa Gozzi of 1989(1).

15. *Il Salvatore della scienza* (Città del Vaticano: Libreria Editrice Vaticana, 1991), in press; Italian translation by Dr. Bruno Bosacchi of 1988(1)

16. Foreword to P. Duhem, *The Origins of Statics* (Dordrecht: Kluwer Academic Publishers, 1991), pp. vii-xv, in press.

17. "Undeceivably Infallible," *The Wanderer*, July 25, 1991, in press.

18. "Meg nem csalható csalatkozhatatlanság," JEL 3/4 (1991), in press, Hungarian translation of 1991(17).

List closed on June 30, 1991.

Index of Names

Abelard, P. 99
Albert the Great 100, 127-128
Alexander, S. 103
Allison, D. C., Jr. 87, 156
Anaxagoras, 25
Antiseri, D., 161
Aquinas, St. Thomas, 19, 39, 42, 48, 60, 69, 99, 108, 148, 159
Aristides, 59
Aristotle, 36, 39, 57-58, 63, 83, 128
Arius, 64, 164
Artigas, M., 156, 168
Ashari, al-, 37
Athanasius, St., 64, 87, 109, 164
Augustine of Hippo, St., 56-58, 60, 147-148
Averroes, 63
Avicenna, 37, 63

Bacon, F., 30, 40
Bacon, R., 88, 100
Baker, K., 133
Barrow, J. D., 94, 149, 158
Basil, St., 58
Bellone, E., 133
Benedetti, G. B., 40
Bergson, H., 103
Blackwell, R. J., 161
Boethius, 57
Bohr, N., 102-103, 159
Bolingbroke, Lord, 82, 154
Bonaventure, St. 60
Bouyer, L., 86, 149, 156
Boyle, R., 40
Bradley, O., 80
Brahe, T., 40
Bridgman , W. P., 101
Bruno, G., 39-40, 84, 138, 141

Budenholzer, F. E., 88, 157, 162
Buridan, J., 37-38, 40, 58, 83-84, 99-100, 106, 141, 155
Butler, S., 112, 166
Butterfield, H., 85
Butterworth, G. W., 147

Calder, P. R., 153
Calvin, J., 109
Carnap, R., 161
Carrel, A., 66
Cauthen, K., 85, 156
Celsus, 56
Chadwick, H., 147
Chesterton, G. K., 18, 62, 111, 166
Churchill, Sir W., 164
Clement of Alexandria, 55
Comte, A., 23, 100, 119
Constantine, 110
Copernicus, N., 28, 38, 40, 69, 155
Copleston, F., 83, 154, 160
Crombie, A. C., 83, 154

Däniken, E. von, 23
Darwin, C., 71-72
Deason, G. B., 84, 155
Denzinger, H., 133
Descartes, R., 31, 40, 42, 67-69, 71, 88, 150
Dewey, J., 13
Dicke, R. H., 145
Dijksterhuis, E. J., 83, 154
Dirac, P. A. M., 27
Drake, S., 147
Duhem, H., 18, 134
Duhem, P., 17-18, 20, 38-39, 83-85, 101, 112, 144, 154, 161
Duns Scotus, J., 99, 108

Eddington, A. S., 14, 102
Einstein, A., 21, 32, 80, 88, 90-91, 102, 104, 153, 163

Fechner, T., 74
Feigl, H., 16, 119, 168
Ferré, F., 118, 168
Fichte, J. G., 31, 70
Foster, M. B., 83, 85, 154
Foxley, B., 151
Freud, S., 74

Galen, 36
Galileo, 38, 40, 57-58, 141, 147
Ghazzali, al-, 37
Giere, R. N., 161
Gilkey, L., 83, 155
Gilson, E., 18, 103, 105, 160, 162
Gödel, K., 26, 47, 70, 75, 145
Goethe, J. W., 23, 25
Gould, S. J., 143
Gregory of Nyssa, St. 58
Guth, A. H., 93

Haffner, P. M., 158
Haig, F. R., 85, 156
Hartree, D. R., 151
Hawking, S. W., 95-96, 107, 122, 159, 164, 169
Hegel, G. F. W., 31, 70, 106, 150
Heisenberg, W., 29, 42, 142, 159
Heitler, W., 16, 134
Helmholtz, H. von, 70
Hendry, G.S. 88, 157
Herschel, W., 28
Hess, V. F., 15
Hippolytus, St., 55
Hitler, A., 79
Hobbes, T., 30
Hodgson, P. E., 13, 86, 90, 95, 156-159, 167
Holton, G., 101
Hooykaas, R., 84, 155
Hume, D., 30, 42
Huxley, T. H., 24, 72

Irenaeus, St., 55

Jaki, S. L. passim
James, W., 13, 103
Jeans, J. 14
Jedlik, A., 14
Jesus of Nazareth, 53, 64; see also Christ, passim
John, St. 54
John Paul II, Pope, 1, 17, 114, 124-130, 133

Kant, I., 31, 40, 43, 45, 69-70, 77, 79, 88, 91, 103, 119, 124, 138-139, 142, 150
Kepler, J.. 21, 40
Klaaren, E. M., 84, 155
Koestler, A., 150
Kuhn, T. S., 23, 31, 80, 84, 101,

Lambert, J. H., 11, 138
Laplace, P. S., 44, 91
Lehmann, K., 135
Lenin, V. I., 23
Leonardo da Vinci,40
Lewis, C. S., 167
Locke, J., 74
Lonergan, B., 103-104, 162
Longley, C., 166
Lubac, H. de, 165
Luther, M., 109
Lyon, J., 162
Lyons, J. A., 165

MacKay, D. M., 84, 155
McLaughlin, P. J., 169
Mach, E., 30, 88, 101
Malebranche, N., 31
Mao Tse-Tung, 35
Maritain, J., 18, 103, 151
Marx, K., 23, 79
Mascall, E. L., 85, 165
Mersenne, M., 30
Messori, V., 133, 171
Mill, J. S., 100-101
Monod, V., 84, 155
Needham, J., 34
Neidhardt, W. J., 89, 157
Newbigin, L., 86, 156

Newman, J. H., 98, 104, 121, 163,
Newton, I., 21, 23, 25, 32, 38, 40,
 58, 88, 90, 100, 104, 136, 141
Nicholas of Cusa, 40
Niebuhr, R., 13
Nietzsche, F., 40

Oddie, W., 156
Olbers, W., 28, 90
Oresme, N., 38, 40, 58, 83–84,
 99–100, 106, 142, 155
Origen, 55–56, 110, 147

Pancaldi, G., 152
Pascal, B., 68, 73
Paul, St. 53–54, 128
Paul VI, Pope, 123–124, 170
Peacocke, A. R., 87, 156
Peter, St., 120
Petry, M. J., 150
Philo, 62–63
Philoponus, J., 57, 83, 155
Pius XII, Pope,15, 121–123, 169
Planck, M., 32, 88, 90, 94, 104
Plato, 59, 99
Plotinus, 106
Poincaré, H., 23, 136
Polkinghorne, J., 159
Popper, K. R., 119, 144, 168
Ptolemy, 28

Rahner, K., 135
Ratzinger, Card. J., 133–134, 171
Reichenbach, H., 161
Ronan, C. A., 84, 155–156
Rousseau, J.-J., 71, 150
Royce, J., 13
Russell, R. J., 159
Russo, F., 119–120, 168
Ryle, G., 150

Sartre, J.-P., 79
Schelling, F. W., 31, 70
Schmaus, M., 109, 164
Schrödinger, E., 27
Seneca, 149
Shakespeare, W., 82

Sharpe, K. J., 86–87, 115, 156, 166
Simpson, G. G., 143
Snow, C. P., 24, 137
Socrates, 25, 154
Solovine, M., 157
Spencer, H., 91
Spinoza, B., 31, 139
Stephen, St. 56
Szabó, G., 14

Teilhard de Chardin, P., 103, 109–
 110, 116, 151, 165
Tempier, E., 38–39, 60, 106
Tertullian, 59, 147
Theodore of Mopsuestia, 57
Theodoric of Freiberg, 100
Theophilos of Antioch, St., 59
Thibodeau, K. F., 89, 157
Thomson, J. J., 27
Tillich, P., 13
Tipler, F. J., 94, 149, 158
Torrance, T. F., 85–86, 156
Torrance, T. S., 89, 157
Tresmontant, C., 164
Trower, P., 135, 162

Vagaggini, C., 19
Von Neumann, J., 73

Weinberg, S., 94, 95, 158
Weizsäcker, C. F. von., 85
Welten, W., 158
White, L., Jr. 165
Whitehead, A. N., 83, 85, 103, 154
Whittaker, E. T., 121–122, 169
William of Champeaux, 99
William of Ockham, 30, 39, 78,
 99–100, 108, 152, 154, 160
Williams, P. L., 166
Witelo, 100
Wittgenstein, L., 31, 75, 102
Wright, T., 28

Young, R. V., Jr., 117, 167

Index of Subjects

age of the universe, 43-44, 91-92, 122-123
animism, 35, 41, 64, 119, 142,
anthropic principle, 44, 46
anthropocentrism, 45, 66, 69
antiscience, 23-24
artificial intelligence 73-76, 102

Babylonian culture and science, 35, 50
beginning, cosmic, 91-92, 94-95, 107, 120-123, 127, 158-159
Big Bang, 124

chance, 42-43
chaos, 71
China and science, 34-35
Christology, 37, 53-54, 56, 62-65, 76, 78-80, 87, 98, 105-113, 164
communism, 22, 34-35, 71, 79
consistency, 39, 167
contingency, 39, 46-48, 92-93, 95-96, 105, 144
cosmic background radiation, 43-45, 60, 82, 91-92, 94-95
creation *cum tempore*, 60-61, 122-123
creation *ex nihilo*, 59-63, 109
curvature of space-time 45

Darwinism, 43, 71-73, 76-79, 117
dualism, anthropological, 65-68, 78-79, 120, 150, 167

ecological crisis, 81, 111, 165-166
empiricism, 30, 67, 69, 100
Enumah Elish, 35, 50-51
eternal recurrences, 18, 34-37, 41, 49-50, 55-57, 63
ethics, 78-81, 111-113, 166

ETI (extraterrestrial intelligence), 23, 76-78, 152
evolution, 66, 71-73, 110
existentialism, 69, 80

Florence, Council of, 107, 163-164

Genesis 1, 50-51, 130
Genesis 2-3, 52
Gödel's theorems, 26, 47, 70, 75-76
Greek science, 35-37, 54

idealism, philosophical, 28, 31, 40, 43, 69-70, 88, 93, 99, 104, 139
impetus theorem, 38, 57-58
instrumentalism, 99
India, ancient, and science 35

Lateran IV, 38, 59, 130, 147-148
logical positivism, 31, 88, 102, 139

Marxism, 22-23, 79
materialism, 30, 71-73, 107
Muslims and science, 37, 106

Nazism and science, 22, 71, 79
nominalism, 30, 39, 78, 99-100, 139

operationism, 24, 43, 101, 104
original sin, 62, 105, 109, 117, 149

pantheism, 36-37, 40-41, 52, 55, 63, 105-106, 128, 140
Planck's time, 94
positivism, 23, 99-101, 157
proofs of God's existence, 42, 99, 109, 118, 122-123, 125

quantum mechanics and objective
world, 27, 42, 94, 102

rationalism, 31, 67–69, 100
realism, philosophical, 18, 32–33,
40, 46–47, 67, 69, 76, 95–96,
103–105, 125, 128, 131, 159,
161–162
relativity, general theory of 45,
82, 91, 94
relativity, special theory of 45,
144
revolution, scientific, 23, 45, 101,
155

science, incompleteness of, 24–29,
94, 112, 124, 126–127, 138;
stillbirths of, 18, 33–38, 82–90,
106; medieval viable birth of,
21, 38–39, 82–90, 98, 110,
128–130, 154
scientism, 22–24, 29, 138
steady state theory, 46, 93, 138,
169

time, 68, 94–95

uncertainty principle, 29, 42, 102,
159

universe, as chief object of
science, 42; as illegitimate
notion, 45, 69, 91; as organism,
25, 34–36, 41, 119; cyclic, 18,
34–37, 41, 86, 108; definition of,
42, 45, 47–48, 105, 127–128;
infinite homogeneous, 28, 44,
70, 91; its emergence out of
quantum mechanical vacuum,
2–43, 96, 130; its unicity, 47, 115,
127–128; oscillating, 46, 145;
specificity of, 44–46, 92–93, 95,
125

Vatican I, 107, 130, 148
Vatican II, 12, 110–111, 124, 168,
170
Vienna Circle, 30–31